Shhh...The Art & Science of Seduction *(& manipulation)*

By

Gregory David

Copyright © 2020 Gregory David

ISBN: 9798666874080

Foreword

To manipulate or not to manipulate...?! Don't we all need to influence those around us from the moment we are born?

Let's assume at that any given moment you want something, even if that is to be left in peace. Let's also assume you don't live alone on an island.

We need to accept that we need people, and what's more people need us! Chances are, whatever it is you want it's going to depend, to some extent, on other people. To get what you want is going to require you to influence people: to manipulate them. To get people, or the person, thinking the way you want them to think and behave as you desire.

The content is an amalgam of twenty five years experience of influencing people plus the study of psychology, behaviourism with the likes of NLP thrown in too. Following is tried, tested and proven streetwise 'know how' coupled with documented science.

This book is going to teach you the fundamentals of human beings: the drivers that make us chose to do the things we do. You will learn how to tune into people and cause them to like you, agree with you and do things you want them to do, willingly!

What those things might be my Libertine....well that's down to your conscience – I can't help you there!

Contents

Chapter 1
The Fabric of a Human

My grandma said to me that if I ever feel frightened of someone I should imagine them sitting on the toilet.

This is a very effective image that I have used several times. Everybody either squats or sits on the loo. There is an important and simple but paradoxically complex message here.

As humans we are the same the World over. There are fundamental factors related to us all that make us tick: that motivate us. We all have the same basic needs. Again paradoxically, they can be our weakness and our strength.

Once you recognise these fundamentals and learn how to evoke them in others, then you can get anybody to do or think whatever you want.

There are some inhibiting features that you must overcome for example, cultural differences, upbringing i.e. environment, and an understanding of where a person is at in their lives; what role they are in. These features will play a part in your ability to influence people but as you become aware of them and accept them, you can adapt. Already you've have moved a step closer to being an influencer!

I read that more money is invested internationally into research about combating hair loss than research into stopping AIDS and Malaria combined.

That resonated with me. We are all self absorbed over and above the greater good, sad to say but true. In fact tests prove that the richer we become the more self serving, arrogant and less charitable we become. Once comfortable we don't reach down to lend a hand, we stamp on their fingers. Although this attitude with education and awareness is reversible, I'm talking about the inner basic instinct. 'Getting what I want comes first and has served me well.'

If we aren't going to decimate this planet then the reversal process must have profit at its heart, in my opinion, or it's doomed. We will consume it by consuming. So therefore what are the dominant drivers of mankind at the moment?

We all very self centred and this seems to be rewarded in modern western culture.

Let's start our journey at the very core of the human being or for now, the core of any mammal.

Question: what is the primary dominant motivator of the behaviour of a majority of people?

I watched a programme about the African plains and the animals that lived on them, as have we all. The cameras were set up around a small watering hole – a big pond effectively. It was clearly a very hot day even for the Africa, let's say 50 degrees centigrade plus. The footage was all about the animals that approached the watering hole and how they behaved. So let's rewind. To continue life firstly we and they need air, then water and then food. So the primary motivator for any one of a number of animals that turned up at this watering hole was? Thirst. Yes, the animals that appeared during the course of the

2

day included; hippos, hyenas, zebras, giraffes, baboons, lions, elephants, etc. They were all motivated by thirst. But how did they behave when they got to the watering hole after what had clearly for most been a long hard trek? They probably felt like speeding up on the sight of it and sticking their faces in the water or just simply jumping in. But they didn't. Not one of them.

So, what was the first thing they made sure of before they even went near to the water, even given that they were desperate for a drink?

Answer: that it was SAFE!

Even the pack of lions checked around with caution before they established an area at the side of the watering hole that they would drink from safely, and they drank with caution in case there were crocs in the pool. The elephants were the same. They checked the situation out, they had a look as to what they might be competing with and made sure their young were safe.

Most people don't take risks because they can. Most people do the same thing over and over, day in day out, week in week out. Yes, we are creatures of habit [more] but we established these patterns primarily because they are safe. We like what we know and we know what we like.

Before people do anything the safety has to be there. How much safety depends from one person to the next. I believe the first thing you must establish with someone if you are going to influence them is safety. Even if you reverse this by positioning your proposition suggesting that they will NOT be safe if they don't take action.

The antithesis and bed partner of safety is fear. Fear is like adrenaline (which supersedes all drugs), it is the first motivator. Fear of a lack of safety.

A whole bunch of people I know spring to mind. They have pretty much lived in the same area all of their lives. Most of them have even lived away from this area for awhile, maybe a few years to go to college for example, but they have returned and are now into middle age and the chances of them moving are slim. This area is not known to be a desirable destination. Successful people in the film industry or wealthy tycoons don't choose to live there.

When I go to visit they tell me about some adventure they've had. This will always be about some travel adventure they've been on. They will get enthusiastic and press upon me to look at photos. The place they visited will be somewhere off 'the beaten track', or so they believe, i.e. somewhere not so mass market, for example southern Spain. They are impressed with themselves because they think they have taken a risk: done something different. This has happened to me several times. Each time I know they have booked the 'adventure' from, in days gone by, a high street tour operator or now an on-line operator, and the whole 'adventure' from the moment they handed their luggage in at the airport has been pre-contrived. It has been made safe. When it was over they went to their safe home and then got up to resume their safe routine (having escaped for a while – but now back to the safe drudgery).

It's ok. We all want safety. We prefer the familiar. We are all wired this way. It is the primary thing we need as children. Take this away and it has severe psychological effects. I know. I am a survivor of familial abuse as a child.

I had no safety and have therefore devised innumerate mechanisms to bring safety into my life. One of them is to get people to do what I want – I attempt to gain control of my environment: gain the control I never had.

I had little safety when I was a child. My need for safety in life is therefore exaggerated and paradoxically my capacity for risk is enormous. Given that I know the extremes I can see clearly the need for safety in others.

Remember that the need for safety is the same as the need respond to fear. Safety is the carrot and fear is the stick.

Know this: the biggest fear people have is that of uncertainty. And the reality is: nothing is certain. Yes the Sun, even if in a diluted form, will come up tomorrow, but you may not be alive to see it. Okay that's uncertainty at its extreme but it's true. As such, people spend their lives looking to establish certainty which is why they like the familiar, we like patterns because it gives us a feeling of certainty, we know what we are going to get and therefore it feels safe.

Let's consider human beings as a creature. Have you watched many wildlife programmes? It would seem that some creatures choose to be on their own and, usually in these circumstances, just one other when they come to mate. Otherwise they live alone. Humans are not like that. We like to gather together; this is 'the herd instinct'. We like people around us generally speaking. It's nice to be alone in peace at times, but on the whole we are social creatures. In fact, it's now recognised that one of the biggest killers is loneliness! And *certainly,* as I will contest on a personal level, becoming isolated is the thing

NOT to do in times when your mental health is challenged despite feelings to the contrary.

There is of course then safety in numbers. If other people are doing it / thinking it, then it's safe. So it's okay. It was okay to go on that 'adventure' because other people had already been on it and other people were going too. So, my goodness it was a risk to go on the adventure, but it was safe because the herd were a part of it.

Have you walked down a street with several restaurants on and one sits empty whilst the next one is full? Sat in an empty cinema or café to have people come and sit near you or start touching the same clothes on the rack you are looking at in the shop?

I call it 'the Osmosis of people', i.e. people devolving toward one another's behaviour.

Besides it being safe because someone else has tried and therefore is already eating the berries / drinking the water at the watering hole and seems okay, therefore the berries, the restaurant, the seats in the cinema are safe, and it also means they don't have to *make a decision.*

The decision has already been made.

People don't like making decisions. Making decisions involves effort. Decisions involve risk. They can involve taking action, making changes and people don't like change because change might not be safe. Change involves moving away from the familiar.

As an aside: the people I have met who are financially successful all make decisions quickly and they make them more frequently than others. This may also apply to other areas of their lives.

Ever walked up to a couple of swing doors that open in the middle? One is closed and the other is open which lots of people are filing through...they wait, queue almost, to get through the open door, they will not try the closed door next to it...why not? Fear. No one else has so they won't take the risk – it also involves initiative which is sparked by a decision. They probably don't even think of trying it. They just follow everyone else: stay with the herd. And/or maybe they don't want to look foolish by trying the closed door only to find it is locked – risk.

But no decision anyone makes is done alone. It is influenced. We do not each live alone. We are being influenced everyday – more than we realise.

And very often a decision someone makes is because someone else has already decided that it is safe. That the decision will lead down the right path.

"yes of course Mr Moneybags, this is most popular option, everybody is very happy with this investment, I wish we could issue more shares in the gold mine in Botswana, everybody wants them...as you know Gold is such a safe investment.."

Here's an interesting concept about the nature of people. I recall watching a programme about how people behave in a crisis. You'll see the best and worst, the extremes of behaviour in these circumstances. One incident was about a plane that crashed on take-off (which I recall them saying was more dangerous than landing). They interviewed surviving passengers afterwards who described how the rear of the aircraft was on fire, smoke was starting to billow down the plane and people were

7

blocking the isle because they were all trying to get their hand language out of the overhead compartments. Pre-programmed herd instinct perhaps? The folk that survived had climbed over the back of the chairs. One chap was saying how people were sat still and someone actually held onto his leg in a kind of 'help me, save me, take me with you' way, and the escaping chap had to kick him in the face which he felt a bit bad about, although probably not as bad as the kicked chap 3 minutes later: choking on smoke with a bloody nose couldn't have been much fun!

The other incident was about a ferry that sank. The back opened up and water flooded in. A chap was saying how he ran into a cafeteria area (these are big on those huge ferries that carry trucks and wot not) and it was full of folk sitting knee deep in water waiting, presumably for someone to tell them what to do. He jumped off and saved himself, he figured a load more would have survived if they'd done the same thing.... Fear of making a decision and taking unfamiliar action.

The experts calculated that only about 4% of people demonstrate initiative in a crisis of this magnitude. There is also evidence to suggest that there is a level of psychopath in us all and the more of psychopath you are, the better your performance in these circumstances. Either way, you're now an innovator, a pioneer and therefore one of the 4%. You are going to lead, because you've already pre-planned what's going to happen. Your prospect is going to agree with you and do your bidding my Libertine.

'That's right Mr.Prospect, you've got it, this way, follow me.'

People want to be told what to do. Enter Libertine stage left.

Recently I had the good fortune to be involved in the debt industry. I thought I knew a thing or two about folk, but how people relate to debt is often odd and particularly devoid of rational thought I have learnt. I have since surmised that we are all deluded. In fact, I heard about a book going round that claims this to be the case, and that if we weren't hope would be extinguished and the suicide rate, for one, would sky rocket. We all live in a state of unreality. But then, isn't the perceived reality, reality? Hmmm.....

'People believe what they want to believe.'

There is a pointer here for the Libertine. Given we are all cursed with hope: if you tune into your prospect you can paint a picture of a better future which they will want to believe. They will even disallow themselves any rational thoughts which may usurp this vision, or find a way of short circuiting them with a delusional thought. We buy primarily with emotions. We are, as humans, a mass of irrational emotions which shift around, I believe, on a minute by minute basis. If the emotions fluctuate as such, (and I read that everything we imbibe generates differing thought patterns and feelings), then it's going to be easy to control the emotions of others by what you say and do and think, i.e. what they imbibe from you: yes?

When in the debt business I was looking for small to medium sized companies that were struggling financially. I was to get in the door, do a fact find and then if they were a qualified prospect pass them on to someone that knew what they were talking about. Great I thought, because I'm a fan of the small business person. In my opinion they should be nurtured because they represent the future of the economy and it's tough for small businesses, with little help or support. I genuinely really wanted to

9

help. I didn't even need the money. Up until the end of the second company I visited I questioned whether I was qualified to be talking to these pioneers who had created a business and had been immersed in their industry/market. I was fine from a business development/sales/marketing viewpoint, but I know little about accounting. There again, I was once involved with a company whose accounts were described by the auditors as being 'managed incompetently', the owner previously having been an MBA lecturer in accounts! Anyway, I realised I had the advantage of common sense acquired perhaps because of my objective perspective. The first hurdle was to get them to admit they had a problem which was getting worse and that they weren't doing anything towards cessation; a case of expecting a different outcome but continuing to do the same thing. Rather like getting the alcoholic in denial to admit they have a problem. Most of them just wanted to borrow more money, i.e. in effect create even more debt under the belief that spending more borrowed money on an unprofitable activity would change it into a profitable one. One of them got some more money and I found out later rather than plug up some of the debt holes, i.e. pay off loans with horrific interest rates and invest in a new area of the business that was showing promise (which we identified), she bought a new car: had really nice tan leather seats though!

My tolerance for some things have depleted with age. In relation to this debt gig and the nature of people I had an epiphany watching a programme about people that hoard (people that fill their house with stuff and never get rid of it). The programme was based around how a specialist psychologist was going to help this unfortunate chap. The two of them crawled around in the house on top of the rubbish stacked virtually to the ceilings by way of evaluating the scale of the issue. Later they sat outside on the kerb and the specialist asked if the chap recognised he had a psychological problem which he denied and countered by stating that he had a storage problem and needed more space! Because the hoarder couldn't accept he had a mental issue the specialist just got up and walked away. I had an epiphany and promptly climbed off the high horse of 'save debt ridden small businesses campaign'. To continue would be collusion and therefore creating my own delusion.

If you can't get a prospect to accept a situation quickly: a state of mind, then move on they are not a prospect. Similarly via my own navigation of mental health: you cannot help those they do not seek it *and* (especially) chose to *take responsibility* for their recovery and change.

So you can help paint a delusion/vision of the future with a prospect, but similarly the prospect may be deluded when you meet them. They may have a false perception of what is out there and how things are going to be. You see this in these property buying programmes and the dating ones too. You've got to ask yourself; is it worth pursuing them, and if so you may have to jolt them quite sharply before you can move the decision making process forward.

It feels safe for them to keep holding the wrong end of the stick. They will most likely vehemently defend their delusion. The delusion will have a moat around it and if you challenge their thinking they will most likely pour boiling oil on you. People have a lot of emotive energy (and often finance) invested in their delusions!

Moral: if they are holding onto the wrong delusion – get ruthless – they'll waste your time.

Another important factor that comes into play when considering the herd instinct is the need for approval. We all have it. We are all influenced by others around us including people we see on the TV, magazines and social media, more than we realise, more than, even if it was pointed out to us, we would like to accept. We are all constantly being influenced by those around us, people in our lives. There is a strong desire to fit in and be approved of and by the same token, to conform. Similarly, approval is the carrot and conformity, or rather non-conformity, is the stick.

When we were children we needed approval from our guardians and later from our peers, from our friends, colleagues and from society.

We need others to make us feel like we are okay and that we belong. This gives us the approval we need. Note: the need for approval is akin to love. They are hard to separate, but the pursuit of unconditional love by one 'adult' for another 'adult' is so infrequently on any agenda that for our purposes we may as well ignore it as a motivation.

The need for approval, to conform, is huge. It is soaked into all of us. It is the main mechanism of a functioning society. In World War one it was found to be advantageous to put soldiers from the same area of domicile together because it made them more loyal: less desertion. They sort after the approval of their peers. We need to feel as though we are part of something: that we fit.

'Hmm, your new car, silver, a good choice.' [safe] (actually I think we are all into white now..)

12

Another paradox of the human is that we are all like finger prints. We all have one and therefore we are the same, but we are all different. Within the herd is a collection of individuals each with their own ego or for our purposes, their soft spot. Whilst the ego can be very useful in so far as it helps people achieve stuff i.e. 'look at me aren't I great', it can also be used like the ring through the nose of a bull.

I get the feeling that a lot of men are particularly susceptible to this next one which is the cousin of approval: the need to impress. It is some man thing about being seen to be macho, the provider, stronger, faster – some basic inner primal feature. Either way, it forms the ring through the bulls' nose and can easily be used to lead people. Some have it more than others. It is something I noticed in myself having gone through a few years of intense self questioning via therapy. I had this constant need to impress because of my negligent childhood. It was a way of attracting some attention and therefore getting a substitute for love. I believe its label is contingency self esteem. Ones' self esteem is contingent on achievement judged by others. I had it bad.

The need to impress, and therefore be validated by our peers: the need for approval.

A lot of women have a similar weakness I believe. I mean, what is it about this seemingly endless supply of females that just have to be on the front of magazines? They just have to be talked about? It clearly becomes an addiction given a good deal of them appear repeatedly. Is there a type of female that devolves towards this need / behaviour? I wonder if most females once exposed to the limelight just don't want to let it go? Either way, it is the need of the flower – the need to be attractive – and again,

13

it in its way, the need to impress, 'look at me – aren't I great!'

In balance: people need to be validated. It is my belief this is why 'selfies' have become so prevalent. A 'selfie', which no one else is interested in looking at, validates the person.

The need for approval and the need to impress exist within us all. You, my Libertine, can learn to find it in your prey and use it to your advantage. Get them wanting your approval and get them trying to impress you, by say….investing in your big idea?!

'My goodness you catch on quick…you know a good opportunity when you see one…'

Another primary motivator is greed. The stock market runs on greed and fear. Try it. I got into it big time and every time you do or don't trade it is fear or greed you are primarily motivated by. So on that note: heard the phrase, 'everyone has a price?' They do. Some years ago I had an acquaintance who was solely motivated by money and he acquired a lot of riches. More begets more when it comes to money. Greedy people never have enough: maybe they are forever trying to fill an empty void. One day they hope it will go beyond a quick hit and they will be satisfied, but more money never does it. Although a multi-millionaire at the cost of his health and well into his twilight years, he still needed to collect more money. His greed took his unbridled attention and justified everything, pretty much any action or attitude to anyone, even his family. My guess is that is there is a deep seated fear greedy people are running from. Notably I observed him buy people and corrupt them. I was often amazed at how abusive he was but people just took it and kept coming back because, every so often, they got money out of him. He attacked his wife and they separated but she continued, and I believe chose, to be in his life because he still brought her money, plus she was embroiled and invested in his corrupt methods. I understand that domestic abuse and the reasons people continue in abusive relationships is complex and has a lot to do with a lack of sense of self worth, which the abuser often perpetuates, but in this case I feel sure it was about money. Perhaps she sold her integrity? Greed knows no bounds.

'God says take what you want, but pay.'

Ever been around or close to someone dying who has money? Since records began people who may well have been close quickly end up hating each other and treating each other with total contempt when it comes to dividing up the spoils. I've witnessed it first hand several times. In fact, it is unusual if benefactors or non-benefactors end up content with the outcome and happily co-existing without resent.

I read once that the cause of all Wars was the desire to commit theft. Greed. Iraq? Oil? WOMD – really?

Most scams are based on greed. They offer something for nothing, or very little. Greed is emotive, it defies logic. We all have areas in our life which answers to greed. Never underestimate how much people will mould their values once greed takes the stage.

I am writing this book because I want it to sell. I want to make money out of it. Clearly, it is not about proving to myself or others that I am a literary genius. It is not about enhancing society. It is about making some money so that my wife and I can live in more comfort without financial worry (safety)…and if I can use it as a platform to make a noise about preventing CSA (childhood sexual abuse – as

15

I was) then great...(I do hope that this is not my ego being the sole motivator, i.e. the need for recognition as the knight/saviour...more a need for revenge and to help others). And in fact, by simply declaring that I am a CSA survivor it helps me and it enables others to speak out, which is therapeutic for one.

Aside on the greed note: this one works 100%. Look out for it. A Japanese psychic told me. People with fleshy earlobes love money. They need money, and they are either good at attracting it or are very careful with it, or both! If you're negotiating with someone with fleshy ear lobes make success based on a win-win because unless yours are too – you're going to lose. Also, Mrs Big Lobes will definitely be attracted by a prospect of more dosh! (If you fall out with a wife with big lobes – she's going to skin you! If he's got small lobes – ding, swipe, next!)

Most aren't totally honest about their motivation. If you are honest about your drivers you will be more impactful as you will see clearly what is motivating and similarly, blocking others.

There are secondary motivators such as shame, which is closely married to guilt. People turn away from shame. They don't want it anywhere near them but, again paradoxically, they keep turning back to it and re-exposing themselves to it. If we want to influence people then projecting shame onto them will not endear them to us. Same goes for guilt. No good making your prospect feel guilty. But the FEAR of both will be a motivator. People don't want shame or guilt. The fear of possessing either will motivate a person. You don't project either on to your prospect: you simply make them aware that there is a potential for either, or both, if they don't make the right decision....

'I suppose it's the dilemma of knowing hooowww... disappointed your wife might feel having to tell her that you got the smaller holiday apartment..'

Power is another secondary motivator. The need for control: the need to dominate. It is in all of us to some extent, but it is my belief that behind the need for power is fear and therefore the need for safety. The need to control others and the need to control one's environment stems from the need for safety. If one has power then the perception is that they are safe.

Power can be linked to conquering uncertainty. Power and therefore control over one's environment gives perceived immunisation against uncertainty. Offering the gain or loss of power when expressing your big idea will indirectly influence your target's need for safety.

Branches of safety in more sophisticated forms are jealousy...or rather, the need for superiority. I personally never suffer from jealousy or its cousin, envy. I can't say why so there is a chink in my armour but I can help you fire it up in others. They are subtle derivatives of fear, ultimately.

What I can teach you though, is how to make your target feel as if they will be able to make others jealous and envious of them. People like this idea. Isn't this one of the cornerstones of social media? – 'I'm doing alright Jack!'

Unfortunately, as human beings we are all tarred with the flaw of wanting to be superior. It makes us feel safe because others are lesser than we are and therefore in a weaker position. Almost as if others provide a cushion upon which we ride. We want others to be weaker and more vulnerable. They will look up to us and admire us and aspire to be like us and be impressed by us. We will therefore be validated and therefore safe. Or so we often think, (hello again Victoria – is that you? Goodness what a lot of handbags, and a happy family, and wonderfully expensive impressive birthday party, and superstar friends, you clever, beautiful, special, interesting, superior, lucky girl, oh how we wish we were you, what an inspiration you are, not a shallow neurotic botoxed bag of insecurity at all: forgive us silly peasants for not loving you more, it's just the weakness of envy that prevents us.....does it ever end?....does that empty void ever get satiated? One more selfie posing with a diamond encrusted handbag should do it...I mean, those foolish women in Africa carrying toxic water about – it's not even branded, eh Kim? – haven't they heard of girl bands,.. can't sing, so what? Eh Chezza?...)

What about the sexual aspect of motivation. Very powerful: the need to express ourselves as sexual beings. The constant need for some females at least, to appear in magazines: the flower that attracts and becomes pollinated, perhaps, as suggested before. Or the man with the big car and is seen as the superior hunter and is therefore more attractive. This is a big subject we will not delve into right now, and for our purposes we do not need to discuss why. But the need to express sexuality: it is hardwired in therefore if your proposition, my Libertine, aligns itself with enhancing your target's sexuality.....good. The expression of sexuality is linked to validation. If someone is a sexual being then they are a valid being, or so they believe.

Despite the female's considerable strengths – hey they must be: they don't enter into this primitive clumsy 'mine is bigger than yours' nonsense that seems to obsess most men in some way or another. Oh no, they have a far more sophisticated variety of weapons. But, a majority of women have a massive Achilles heal and that is......they are

18

suckers for CHARM [more later]. Being a kind, considerate, thoughtful, flattering, chatty, listening chap goes along way.

As do a couple of other things....money and power.

A couple of in-depth books I read on anthropology came to the conclusion that women (heterosexual) will more happily share the wealthy powerful man than choose to have a monogamous relationship with a poor man. Current (formed in the last couple of thousand years) social morays, including the widely accepted morals of Christianity, protect the poor man and enable him to get a mate. Add in that it is proven that women rarely 'marry down', i.e. rarely marry a man whose 'status' is seen as lesser than their own. I suggest that it is comfort and safety provided by the superior hunter image that is at the core of their decision making when it comes to the mating game, and therefore influences a good number of their decisions. On a basic level, which says a lot, rarely does a female want a male that is shorter than they are or will even consider a man that is. Oh yes, they want a soul mate as long as.....he's powerful, rich, famous and tall, but hey, not necessarily in that order.

I mean, how many responses do you think a dating ad like this would get?

'Man aged 89, 5'2", average looks WLTM beautiful tall female aged under 45 for long term relationship and procreation.' Not one is my guess. Unless they added in that they are a billionaire! 'Eh, Bernie?'

Men simply want to spread their seed. There is evidence which concludes that men just want to shag around. They want, via some mechanism, to express their 'manhood'. That 'mechanism' may be a variety of things beyond what car they drive. Conversely, most men in my opinion do not grow up. I have only just crawled into adulthood recently in my mid 50's. Most men marry their 'mum' (a replicate) and need looking after. Again, safety.... be attractive and mate with lots of women....and still be able to go home to mum, err I mean partner...

As a caveat, rather like Freud who *I understand* (could be wrong) after all his conclusions and observations which have formed the basis for understanding and, at the least, have provoked argument around the issue of human behaviour and psychology if not formed cornerstones in these academic endeavours, ended by more or less saying 'none of the above applies to the Irish..'. I am also making sweeping statements and observations which do not include the gay community. Not by way of conscious prejudice (in fact I get on really well with both gay females and males, especially lesbians – might dig around in the psyche about that one sometime), just the variety ignorance created by lack of knowledge/experience.

A further controversial aside whilst I'm at it: I have this theory that women don't have friends like men do, only close rivals. They never really trust each other. More than men, women will slit another's throat to get what she wants. I read an article suggesting that women in positions of power in male dominated environments do not help the fellow females up the slippery slope – the opposite in fact!

I may have painted a dark picture as to what motivates us my Libertine but this isn't about judgement: I am not judging, i.e. saying what is right and wrong. I am just offering observation as to what people do and why, which often boils down to very basic core animal like drivers.

People are actually very simple and, in fact, very fragile.

Chapter 2
A Frame of Mind:
The Libertine

So that's them my Libertine, now let's think about you. Let's work out what needs to be in your mind: what attitude you need to get the target to do what you want.

Before we go any further you need to know this: people need to be exposed to an idea five times before they will own it. This means that whether it's a product or an action, or a concept that you want people to adopt and therefore they have to make a decision, they need to be exposed to the idea five times. This applies absolutely in influencing. Even subliminally the person needs to experience five exposures. No matter how persuasive you think you are you will not sell a brand new Yacht for a tenth of its value in an afternoon – even a yacht salesperson would struggle. People have to have their minds moulded. You have to create desire first, or find people with the right desire at that moment and then build trust – all this takes several exposures. So bear this in mind when you are looking to influence someone. Bite size chunks at a time. Let me say that the 'five times' may not necessarily be direct contact from you. You may plant the idea and then they pick up exposure/information from other sources.

Let's start at the beginning.

Let's think about what is going to happen. You are going to get someone to *tip over,* i.e. make a decision and do something. So the first key thing is that you have to have decided with absolute clarity is; what it is what you want them to do? You have to fix that in your mind. You need to have that clear picture in your head. Ultimately, you are going to paint that picture into theirs. You must have already made the decision for them. You must have a clear path in your mind. You must have unwavering certainty. From a position of unwavering certainty you can manoeuvre your target into doing what you want. Because if you are more certain than your target then they will, one way another, capitulate and do your bidding! Or moreover, their wobbling track will cross yours several times but with your certainty their track will, in time, blend with yours almost as if magnetised. In essence, it becomes easier for them to do so rather than resist.

During the journey with your prospect you will always maintain certainty. This is not about being overly direct, or pushy, or dominant, it's about you keeping a clear picture in your mind.

You may not paint the picture in their mind in one go. In fact, it will probably be detrimental if you do. You need to build it, sketch it out, paint in the background etc.

What it is you want them to do is down to your conscience my Libertine.

I caste my mind back over the times when I've been very successful at selling, of which there have been many, and I concluded that it's about *expectancy*.

Without dissecting the detail just now of my tactics; in essence I no longer pushed. When I became successful in my mind I was already at the sale; part of me was beyond it. The person had already accepted my idea even before I had spoken to them.

I used to sell computer contractors into jobs. In my imagination I would be visiting them at the company, at a later date, and they'd be doing the job I'd got for them and both parties (company and candidate) would be happy. I'd be getting referrals too; chatting with the other contractors in the same office that didn't belong to me, handing out them my card. Before this conclusive situation my conversation at the outset with the contractor, and subsequently the client, would have been littered with references to how things will be in the future. How much better off they will be, how it's been for others and how normal it all is. I'd paint a picture of the future in their minds. I'd get them to own the new, better future.

I'm not pushing them towards something. I'm inviting them to join in. I'm magnetising them.
Push people and their natural reaction is push back.

'He was too pushy.' They'll find a way out. They'll avoid you.

The path has already been trodden. It is safe.

And I'll tell you another interesting discovery I experienced. If you paint a picture of a brighter future for them, they naturally begin to have negative feelings about their current situation. They become discontent with their existing 'safety'. They want change.

I my more ruthless days in the personnel/recruitment business I used to find the names of people in jobs in my area of expertise – computer sales people. I had a way of getting the receptionist to give me names with a deliberately convoluted spiel about having been asked to pass on a new tennis racket I'd recently bought for a friend of mine who'd asked me to buy it for a friend of theirs who worked there in sales but my friend had been called away because of a family issue...(got it? no? neither did the receptionist..)...and I haven't got their name and I thought I'd get it to them and who do you think it would be? And the I would profile the person I was looking for..

" She's about 26...I know she's been there for more than two years..' (that looks better on the CV)...

And bingo, the receptionist would list the names: Roxy?'...'Err...no..., doesn't sound familiar.'. 'Susan?'...'Errr no ...' etc.

Then I'd call back the next day with a slightly different accent asking for them directly 'Susan please,...yes, she knows me, we've spoken before, yes just pop me through please..' [tell them].

'Hi Susan, we haven't spoken before but I operate in the business of placing the top performers in your field and I've heard some great things about you...I know it may be difficult right now...but I have an exceptional opportunity I wanted to pass by you, you may be interested or perhaps you know someone that might..'

'... well Susan, if you were to give me a name you'd want me to respect your confidentiality...so I can't say who gave me your name.'

Bam. The hook goes in the mouth.

I would slide in then out and I promise you they wouldn't even remember my name, and certainly not the company I worked for, few asked. They became all of a flutter. I cite 'Susan', just so for the guys too.

The 'exceptional opportunity' was exceptional of reality – it didn't exist.

24

Whooah, suddenly there's another better World out there. They are wanted: in demand. Someone else wants to love them the way they deserve to be loved…!

I'd get them in to visit me 'for a casual chat'. They'd come in all sheepish and guilt ridden like they were going to a sleazy motel for their first extra marital encounter. I'd have no papers or pen. We'd just chat and I'd outline this 'exceptional opportunity' and ask gently if I could mention them and their background – not their name or where they were…just offer my client a 'taster'.

Then I'd wait. And in that time the seed would start to grow and discontent for their existing situation would ferment, and so would excitement for the future. At the same time I would know that the idea of change at this stage is premature. So after a while, [I developed an instinct for the time period] in fact they'd often contact me, I would gently let them down. Take it away from them.

'..hmm this one is not going to go our way this time…not to worry, I'm having a lunch week after next and I've a feeling they've had some new investment…I think this could be a better fit'.

Trust me my Libertine, within four months, every time, they'd be phoning me up. I'd put them on hold for a little while.

'Greg please help me, get me out of here!'

Then I'd list the conditions as to how 'we' were going to operate, e.g. what they would say in the interviews, how they would contact me immediately on getting out, etc, etc.

And then later.. 'oh I heard on the grapevine that one of your salespeople just left, it's just that I had a chat with a top performer the other day who expressed some discontent, but if he's going to move he'll get offers

25

quickly, you'll need to chat with him sooner rather than later..'

Wicked little Gregory buying nice clothes and dining in good restaurants an' all! Hey, just giving the merry go round a little push!

(maybe ol' Kris is right, f*k what other people say, think of the money!)

People are creatures of habit. We know what we like and we like what we know. We like something new as long as it's similar to what was before. You're in the business of making people change. To help them do this you have to project them into the future, the new better future – the new safer, better future.

The 'yes I'll do it' from the target shouldn't be thought of as a big build up to a crucial, and therefore highly pressured moment, like the build up in a classical musical piece to a crescendo. No, it becomes smoothed over; the 'yes' is part of an assumed on-going process from the moment you meet them.

I wasn't pushing people into the unknown, i.e. the punter being herded reluctantly into a pen. I was guiding them towards where I was already waiting. I was luring.

In summary: the start point is A and the end point is B. B is not them saying 'Yes' to "will you order today?" B is not them writing a cheque. B is them enjoying the benefits of what you can do for them. You have B painted in your mind. You're going to help them paint it in theirs. But know this: you are going on the journey with them, this journey of information gathering and choice making. It's a fresh new journey every time. It's not trotting out some well worn pitch in hope it sticks! You are going on the journey of five exposures with them almost with the same sense of wonder. NOT with a tone of impatience or unenthusiastic 'take it or leave it' lethargy – they will most probably leave it....although lethargy is not to be confused with nonchalance, which can be very powerful. There is something very alluring about that casual nonchalance....'I've done this before,' calm confidence, 'the sun is shining on me already, come and join me why don't you?'

But before you take the minimalist approach you have to really know your onions i.e. know your game, because nonchalance mixed with not knowing what you are doing equals incompetence in the mind of your prospect, and that won't be forgiven.

Surely, the expectancy concept is nothing new. It is a key part of sports psychology. Don't coaches get sportspeople to picture success in their minds first: train their brains to accept success? The athlete may well picture the ball going in, hitting the back of the net, the dart hitting the spot, picking up the trophy? It's recognised that the success of professional tennis players is 40% mental. How about picturing that boss giving a pay rise, hey, he soon will be! Or that young handsome chap with the inheritance going on his knee and opening that little box?

In summary: the key element to influencing people is to make them feel safe with you. In order to feel safe they must trust you. The first thing you must establish and therefore maintain throughout the relationship is trust. Once trust is established people will follow your lead. Your lead is inhabited at its core by the decision you have already made. That decision is what you want them to do.

27

What you want them to do has already, i.e. at the start of the relationship, been painted clearly in your mind with certainty.

You are going to project the idea that is in your mind into theirs and they are going to own it and act on it.

Ever heard of 'clustering'? How people around us, and when I say 'around' given the Internet these people may be physically remote, influence us and how we affect them and how significant this is. How our physical weight, for example, can be influenced by peers who in turn were influenced by others. There's a science behind this clustering concept which is used to change the sections of society's behaviour by influencing certain members of a cluster, or nodes as they were called, i.e. key influencers within a cluster.

It is safe for them to be a part of a cluster. And clusters have influencers. Think how successful influencers are on social media.

Think of yourself as a node: a key influencer, my Libertine.

When it comes to decisions, 'people like what they know and know what they like.' I can't count the number of times I'd be pitching for marketing campaigns and the prospect would say at fact find stage, 'we want The Benetton campaign'. At that time Benetton were doing a very controversial campaign; pictures of Aids victims in their last days etc. They never took one. I'd show them three and they would always take the safe option. We had a bunch of Benetton type ads which we just changed a bit and wheeled out at each pitch knowing we'd never use them. Obviously, they would then miss the first important point of advertising i.e. attention, (AIDA – attention, interest, desire, action). Better take the safe option then! And so they'd project their own fears into the profitability of the company; to the detriment.

The point I'm getting to here is that people evolve towards what is safe; what other people are doing/ wanting. You have to create the impression that what you have is different, better, exclusive, but conversely it's what others want and what other people are doing, others want this and you are busy giving it to them. 'If you want something doing give it to a busy person'.

You are always busy my Libertine. You always have something to do, people to see, stuff going on in your life (even if you haven't). You have 'an energy' around you. You talk often of something 'a good friend said', you are often complimentary about people you know; you talk about 'how you are so inspired by so & so...', 'you admire the way they get on with things and make decisions without messing about...'. You transmit an air of being in demand, of being popular. Other people will then magnetise to you. They will want to impress you. They will feel reassured by the positive way you talk about people and they want this to be them, they want to believe that you will talk about them positively in their absence. So they listen for clues as to how to behave around you. Remember: always be positive!

I met a chap who was a grifter. He lived off everyone around him. I heard he went on a golfing holiday having 'forgotten' his money and had to borrow off his 'mates' whom he never paid back. For the price of a cup of coffee I spent sometime with him and noticed how he spoke so highly of his 'good friends', how a 'good friend' had done this or that for him...somehow I felt myself wanting to be considered one of his *good friends* and wanting his approval, I wanted to be spoken about like that. But I'm tight – I creak when I walk – tighter than my need for approval and so made a point of reminding him that he owed me a coffee every time I saw him – just for the hell of it – he avoided me (not a good target for him).

Ever heard that one about getting rid of someone? Lend them some money!

Have you ever looked round and focused on someone's eyes that are looking at you? Conversely, have you ever been looking at someone and they have flicked their head round and looked you directly in the eye?

A chap I knew who was into shooting animals (not my thing) told me that he would see a deer and lift up his gun, position it under his chin whilst looking at the middle distance to the side of the animal. When he was ready to pull the trigger he would focus his eyes on the target at the last instant then shoot. He'd done this a lot and found that if he looked at the animal whilst positioning the gun it would go, not so if he didn't look directly at it before he positioned the gun.

So, suddenly looking round into someone's eyes because there's a genetically inherited survival instinct kicking in: we are being hunted, which makes sense. But what is transmitted? What is the energy that goes from one person to the other? The person looks round at you focusing absolutely and immediately on your eyes. Think of the literally infinite number of positions you can focus on within your scope of peripheral vision even without moving, up close right out to the horizon. If we could recognise and harness that energy! When it happens to me I try to be conscious of it, although the occasion always catches me by surprise. The best I can do so far is to detect a warm feeling on the side of my head that originally was turned towards the person looking at me. And similarly, I find that if I look at the side of someone's head and *judge them* they look around immediately.

This transmission, or energy, is de-codable by all creatures. We all have it. What is it? It's intuition, but how does that work then? What is the currency? Dogs, for one, feel it instantly and are well attuned to it.

We know nothing.

'You could feel an atmosphere'.

When we are with someone/s there is a lot of non-verbal communication, beyond body language. I think there are transmissions between people's minds. In relation to influencing without speculating on something I know little, i.e. how we think (I'm not sure anybody does), I'm talking about projecting a vibe. You project a vibe with the thoughts in your head – the feelings you have. You therefore have the choice to employ some self talk, or visualisation. Isn't it possible to alter your thoughts from beta to an alpha state with thoughts *you chose* to have: throw in some deep breathing perhaps? With these thoughts you can pump up your positive energy which will be transmitted. What is more, and here's the important bit, you can create a feeling of certainty and you can **project the energy of certainty**.

The person with certainty is hard to beat, they are more likely to get their way. When you meet that prospect or call them, your certainty that they are going to agree with you must be absolute. They meantime, have all sorts of often unrelated thoughts spinning in their heads. When you have certainty you can handle their objections, close them down, tell them to do it. You can easily let them go off on a tangent and not worry because the hook is in them; the lure will wear them out and you will reel them in and get them back to the big idea, that big idea full of certainty. You have the net result firmly pictured in your mind, them as a happy customer. They will feel it. They will see it in your eyes. They will hear it in your voice. They will succumb to it. To you, doubt does not exist.

And further; that 'energy' the one you send saying 'it's ok, do it' goes into their heads. Prove me wrong. What's that about a great chess match where one of the players complained that he thought several in the audience had been employed to stare at him; he suggested that they were transmitting a negative vibe. Whether they were or not it worked, he lost.

Try thinking 'I love you, you are beautiful' when you look at people. Just try it. You'll notice a change in the way people treat you. They will like you.

What about confidence?

You're going to need confidence my Libertine.
I know I project the persona of someone who has self confidence.
Let me tell you right now no matter what your circumstances are, what you look like, your background, your education, etc, etc..you can have confidence. And it's easier than you think.

Never mind all the deep therapy.

You can generate confidence with just a few easy steps.

Confidence is ethereal. It can come and go in an instant. One day you can feel confident about things, the next you are not. You may be confident about doing some activities: in fact, it's not being arrogant it's just that you've done them lots of times before and so you don't analyse them too much, but there are other things you are not so confident about. Some people seem to be confident about some things, probably because they are used to them, but you can be sure they are not confident about others. Take anyone out their comfort zone and they lose confidence. I recall seeing a programme about reviewing cars where one of the hosts drove his mother around a circuit in a fast car – she was terrified, and he seemed amused by this. Then he had a turn in a bobsleigh; when the 'run' had finished he couldn't talk and walked away from the camera because he was so disturbed by the level of fear he had felt.

All this to say: we are all the same. We have patches of confidence and patches of the opposite.

The solution? Fake it.

Confidence can be faked. And you know what? That is how you become confident. Well it is one of the ways. The other is to do the thing that you fear over and over. But we don't have time just now.

So let's fake it until we make it. Literally.
Act confident and you know what? Confidence comes in like that ethereal wind that it is and fills the gap.
So, think about your posture. Is it upright and straight backed? Is your chin up (straight ahead – not raised, i.e. nose in the air). You know that your physiology dictates your mood and therefore your thoughts (which are very fickle)? If you are acting confident then your mind gets

the message that you are confident and begins to send confident thoughts, then a cycle begins. It actually takes conscious effort to have negative self defeating thoughts if your back is straight, your shoulders are pinned back, your head is up and you are looking forward.

Then have a conscious think about your mannerisms. Simple, bold, open gestures, but controlled – cut the hand waving and equally, the overly servile look, i.e. hands clasped in front of you.

Have a listen to your voice tone too. We'll talk more about this. Slow down your speech. Don't gibber. But use interesting inflection, i.e. not monotone. **And don't 'errrr'.** Speak clearly and concisely. Great influencers were very often good orators. You can learn.

Above all: make the effort to be a positive person. I mean, 'make the effort'.

First step: make the decision!

Chapter 3
Mirror Mirror on the Wall...

If your target trusts you they are more likely to believe you. They'll forgive you if you make mistakes. They'll even cover them up for you. They will defend you.

So, who is the person they most feel comfortable with? Which person is the one they feel is the most important? Who is the person they feel the safest with?

Themselves!

So if you want the target to trust you, you need to look like them and behave like them. Notice married couples, they often look like brother and sister. It's said that people look for their mirror image, or marry someone that looks like a parent. Back to the safety thing!

So let's explore body language.

It is also widely accepted that as humans we share a lot of behavioural similarities, even despite cultural differences. Adopting the right behaviour at the right time sends signals to the recipient. We can therefore control the subliminal signals we send to our target.

Also, we each have our own patterns of behaviour, facial expressions, gestures etc, which keenly observed can de-code what is in the person's mind and how they feel. One of my mates once said that if you live with a woman long enough they know what you're thinking before you do. But beware clumsy assumptions based on what you see when watching another person. There is the danger of isolating a gesture or pose and then not seeing past it. This can lead to false conclusions. I suggest, my Libertine, you add gestures with expressions and what is said together. Put the elements into clusters. It takes practice.

Also of importance is the fact that you will learn how to spot when people aren't telling the truth. Unless you are dealing with a psychopath who has no conscience and is therefore dissociated from their feelings, and even then there will be 'tells'. When lying we give ourselves away because lies create physiological outputs. We're going to learn how to read them. This is key because you can be sure that the phrase 'all buyers are liars' has a lot of truth in it. In order to influence your prospect you will need information from them, and you will need to check en route how they are feeling about your proposition.

Let's start with gaining trust, which I will return to again later.

Note that we all judge people. What's more we judge people very quickly. As soon as we meet people we make a judgement. In fact, we make several almost instantaneously including; status, wealth, health, sexuality, confidence etc, and we decide whether or not primarily if a person is safe. Can we trust them? Are they friendly? Are they a threat?

First impressions count. On meeting people we make a host of judgements and once made we then look to reaffirm them. Folk look and listen for reinforcement of the judgement they have made about you. It is a safety mechanism to do so. People will put a label on you as fast as they can: immediately. If they've put a label on you they know what kind of person you are and therefore they feel safer.

Heard the phrase 'oh so you're a (*this-or-that*) kind of a person'

What's more, people don't like to be proved wrong or admit even to themselves that they are wrong. This applies to all decisions we make. People are quick to get hold of an 'end of a stick' and loathe letting go. So, make a bad first impression and it will stay with you.

Let's start with the greeting. This may be the first or the seventh.

A simple way of establishing that you are safe trustworthy person is to transmit this with your stance and facial expression. Obviously a tooth displaying smile is good but it must be a 'real' smile therefore you need to make sure it's not a coat hanger smile, i.e. one that looks like you've stuck a coat hanger in your mouth. The corners of your mouth need to be turned up and you need to smile with your eyes too, i.e. the corners of your eyes need to be creased (eh Duchess?). Watch out for forced smiles. When someone gives one to you I suspect that it will actually give you an unpleasant sensation.

The smile should also be accompanied by direct eye contact. Practice looking into people's eyes [more], especially when you first meet them. Accentuate the whole experience with an eyebrow lift – not just a flash – keep them raised along with the smile for a minimum of three seconds.

The stance should be open, especially the midriff region. Keep the midriff area fully exposed (not naked), i.e. don't put your hands in the way. Got a belly issue? Deal with it: either get rid or get over it. At first keep it flat on, which is directly in front of your target. If you're wearing a jacket open the buttons. The hands should be in full view and, if possible, splay them out to your side with the palms facing your target.

'Hey look, I'm unarmed.'

This way your prospect will instantly take you in at a glance and see that you are friendly and safe. This impression will stick. From then on they will align as much as they can in terms of what you say and do with you being safe, friendly and trust worthy. They will make an immediate judgement and will simply keep adding confirmation with further evidence that reinforces it. It works in reverse if you do the opposite.

So, make the effort. Get in the habit. First impressions count. Do this routine every time you meet someone. Try it with everyone. Before you know it people will be labelling you a 'nice, warm, decent person' my Libertine...

Let's look more at body language. Be aware that we share the World over many behavioural characteristics but again, beware of assumptions. As a general rule, again, look for clusters.

For example, it's a generally held belief that if a person's arms are folded they are having negative thoughts. It is often seen as a barrier.

'I'm not buying any of your bullsh@t!'

Sort of, but for me on the rare occasions I fold my arms I'm re-absorbing and collating information, you may find you're the same. Keep talking at me and chances are I'll get irritable.

If a prospect has been happily talking to you and they fold their arms, especially if they look away, you may have lost them, but most likely they are relating what you have said to their world. Best you shut up; even ask them what they are thinking, even if you have to break your own flow; stop mid sentence.

"**May** I ask....how do you feel?" and shut up.

Most amateur Libertines feel compelled to force their target to listen to them, turn up the volume for example – wrong.

The folded arms aren't necessarily a negative they are effectively a self hug. They may be hearing information (especially if they stare at you at the same time) that is having a strong impact on them. Rather than rejecting what you are saying they have to hold themselves because it is affecting them. Being earnest is your best approach here: clear, steady and concise. Forget the games show host persona for now.

As I have been writing a plumber has been trying to fix our old boiler. He stepped away and looked at me solemnly and began to explain the problem. Whilst he did I noticed I had my arms folded which is rare for me. I was keen to hear what he had to say although I didn't want to hear it! I had a reality to face and he was delivering the facts of life – the boiler was dead. I was listening intently, *trying* to accept what he was saying and I was self hugging.

Back to the standing communication: you've done your open greeting. Great, here's the warm, nice, pleasant person, now what?

Keep your hands in view, i.e. not behind the back and, if you can, practice standing with your hands by your side when with people. It feels unnatural but it doesn't look unnatural. Even better, try talking with your hands by your side, this feels really odd but again, it doesn't look odd at all. It is something that actors learn to do – look out for it.

Also, when sitting down with your prospect always keep your hands in view. Do not speak to them, especially, with your hands out of sight under the table. Keep your hands apart on the table, and still. Try listening to someone when their hands are hidden, if you tune into your feelings they will be on alert; you won't feel comfortable with the person or with what they are saying.

This next bit is key:- if you are a man talking to another man, as soon as you can stand to his side. If you are talking to a woman, stay standing in front of her. And vice verse: if you are a woman talking to a man stand at his side, and if talking to another woman stand face to face. Why? Because men are pack animals and if you stand in front of them they see you as a challenge. They feel more comfortable if the person who they are talking to stands side on. Women are the opposite, they stop trusting the person they are talking to if they stand at the side of them. They can't fully see you and they don't like it, especially if you are a man. Don't believe me? Try it. I guarantee you will have a different physical sensation when you swap around what are four permutations. As a man it will feel uncomfortable: threatening if you stand face on. I bet your heart rate goes up which you will transmit. You will also notice how the other person reacts differently to you.

If you are a woman talking to a man, stand at his side. It will feel odd but you are sending the message that you are in his pack, that you are there to support him.

Same goes for sitting. If I'm with a female I will sit opposite and remain so, square in front of her. With a man I will twist, move my chair if possible: swivel and push one arm forward on the table and the other back and hook my elbow over the back corner of the chair (keeping my hand in view). The arms will remain open – not going across my body.

Go to a bar or a place where people are static, talking to each other. Those that are getting on will be mirroring each other, subliminally; they're not doing it consciously. They simply feel comfortable with one another.

I'm not talking about being Marcel the silent clown that matches everything someone does. If they cross their arms, cross your legs. Do gestures that are not exactly the same but are similar. Again, beware, don't mock.

Trick: when you're saying something and you get to the vital bit, touch your heart just briefly, then swing your arms out a little with your palms turned forwards, lower your tone, make it intimate, serious, just for them. Lean forward a little, appeal to them. This transmits that you are speaking from the heart, it works. Don't overdo it!

Always maintain eye contact or, at least, keep going back to looking your prospect in the eye. This transmits respect. Sometimes though, it can be difficult if not awkward to keep staring your prospect in the eye, somewhat intimidating for both of you. A simple rule here is the eye triangle. If the situation is business like then imagine a point between your prospect's eyes but raised a little, and move your gaze on to one eye, to the middle point and then to the other eye then back again. If the situation is more personal then use the middle of the target's top lip as your focus point and then again, from the one eye to the lip and on etc, eye to eye...This can be very seductive.

Another *trick* is to throw in a bit of vulnerability here and there, especially if you feel you've been overdoing the wide stance with the hands on the hips approach: try the ear tug. A tug of the ear when your talking gives off a subliminal message that you are safe, okay, a nice person, fallible.

Think about this one: you are going to get someone to make a decision and make a change / take action. How's your decision making going? I find that if things aren't happening in my life it's because I'm stuck. It's probable that I'm not making decisions about things, or a thing. If you're not making decisions in your life and therefore you are not moving then it is likely that you will transmit this. You will, almost at a subliminal level, provide the opportunity for the prospect not to make a decision. You will unwittingly give them an out. To combat this you must be sure that your life is moving along. Be sure that at a basic level you are making quick decisions about the little stuff, for example. This is a good place to start. People that stand around in supermarkets staring bewildered at products will not make good influencers. Make sure you are not one of these people.

"oo eerrr, cheese or egg roll...errrr...are the eggs fresh eggs...errr..what type of cheese is it...errr... do you have sandwiches...?' – get the F on with it!

Overall, in summary you are looking to be confident but not threatening. At the same time behave like them without them realising you are doing it, because if they do they will see that you have got something up your sleeves my Libertine. This can be a difficult balance.

Chapter 4
Telling Porky Pies

Lying – 'The lady doth protest too much, methinks'

Let's think about lying and behaviour. The reason being: it's very useful to spot if someone else is lying and it means that you can control yourself my Libertine (should you need to – I mean, that little porkie might be for their own good of course! Do they really need to know you haven't got a licence, or you were acquitted in the re-trial given that the witnesses changed their statements?).

There are all sorts of statistics on how often people lie. In fact, it's several times a day. And if my memory serves me correct, females start earlier and are better at it (we may think we are the stronger sex but they know they are).

So here we are lying a lot! Not only lying externally (to others) but lying to ourselves too, and we won't admit it or even allow ourselves to be aware of it. In fact, I believe it's proven that we need to be at least partially deluded about stuff in order to continue.

It takes a trained eye to spot when someone is lying. Again, I'll use the phrase clustering. Look out for clusters of behaviour and verbal 'tells' too. They'll be there because, for proven scientific reasons, when we tell a lie it affects us physiologically; heart rate shift, chemicals being released into the body and so on. Bottom line for 99% of us when we lie we are affected and we give out 'tells' i.e. signals. Like poker players – the successful ones remain stony faced and stay still – hence 'poker face'.

When people lie it's in the first five seconds before or after they will most likely give you the 'tells'. One of which will be a pause after you've asked them a question. You see my Libertine, lying is harder work for the brain than telling the truth because people have to invent stuff. So if they pause before the answer it's likely they are imagining the answer.

Another potential myth, for example, 'if they touch their face they're telling a lie'. Is it as simple as that? Is that always true? I think a lot of people believe this one, so avoid touching your face as they might think you are lying. But, if they touch their face when talking to you then view it in conjunction with what they are saying (tone / manner [more]) however, red flag whatever they are saying, i.e. it is more likely to be an untruth because, if you hadn't already guessed, they are trying to hide from you....but, if they rub their eye after you have asked them a question and before they answer, it means they don't like what you are asking them. They are struggling with it. A lie is probably on its way.

Why will they touch their face? If they lie the resulting chemicals released will cause them to want to itch and as such it may cause them to touch their face, or scratch, or shift uncomfortably, either way it is likely to make their face redden, plus their eye movement will change and they will look away *or* stare at you fixedly in a challenging fashion – observe their eye movement [more]. So, touching their face in conjunction with other 'tells' (clusters) - redflag.

A lot of the clues will be in their dialogue. Following is a quick fire list -

'..err, well, not really' or '..for the most part' – being vague in an answer, or more specifically attaching nebulous phrases to the answer. This is way of not committing to the answer. They are looking to skip the detail. It usually means they are leaving something out of the answer, or rather, not giving you the straight answer. In the same way they are afraid of lying directly so they try to dilute what they are saying: being non-committal.

If someone is lying they know it and will try to hide it. They may well become theatrical.

If they are aggressive in answering you and trying to be intimidating, they are trying to scare you off. They may behave like this after they have made a statement and then go on to defend it aggressively, coupled with attacking you. The best way of defence is attack and this is what they doing: deflecting by attacking. This is different to being genuinely angry which a person may be if they are telling the truth and are feeling indignant. If they are lying the anger will be more theatrical. It is designed to put you off. Real anger possesses people and they are likely to say things that are inappropriate, or they may struggle to articulate what they are saying; they may well splutter and choke trying to get their words out. When people are being 'theatrically' angry they can still articulate and they will over emphasise what they say.

Are they theatrically infuriated throughout your questioning? They have adopted a mode, i.e. being infuriated, and they don't stop throughout their story or through the answers to your questions. The infuriated mode is a smoke screen.

If they are telling the truth they will be angry in flashes. It will not be a consistent flow.

46

Equally, being over relaxed – attempting to brush you off. They are hiding something. They are hoping that you will adopt the same lack of concern and move on.

"Oh I don't really know…I'm not really bothered…oh, don't worry about that."

By contrast: inappropriate level of concern: being overly surprised or excessive frozen frowning.

"Nooo, reallllY!!.....Oohh, your kidding me!!....Whaat! They said I spent the money, noooo."

Theatrical!

When people tell the truth they deny directly and simply. "No I didn't."

People don't like to falsely deny something directly so they talk around the subject if they are lying and make a great effort to convince you.

"Ahhh, the sweating, ahh now it's interesting you should mention that because I couldn't have been sweating because you see, I had this issue with the fact that I was shot at in the Falklands war, and blah, blah…", and into some pre made up complex story which is supposed to be convincing.

Rather than, " what, a, load, of, rubbish." The end.

If they're lying they try and convince you. They try to sell you the story.

"I swear on my….". They're lying. Be very suspicious if they start to swear on things.

"To tell you the truth…If I'm honest with you…..Well frankly…", the next bit is, or was, very possibly a lie.

Over talking:- when people tell the truth they don't worry about specific details. Memory comes back in lumps and people connect events in an often disjointed fashion. But, if they are lying they may well have a pre-planned answer full of detail, and they will over talk. If they know in advance that you are going to ask them about something that you suspect they will lie about they have time to plan a lie which will be full of detail, which they have rehearsed in their minds. When they 'trott it out' it will be as though they reading from a script. If you ask a related somewhat off track question, their speed of delivery, pitch etc will change, they are now off-script and they have to think.

Ever seen 'Reservoir Dogs' (which in my opinion remains the best Tarantino movie) when an experienced policeman is training another to be an undercover cop. By way of establishing his credibility with the gang of baddies prior to his infiltration the experienced officer gives the rookie a pre-scripted story to tell the gang about his previous brush with the law. When the trainee practices the story the experienced policeman keeps interjecting with related but off track questions. The experienced policeman knows that if the new guy stumbles on the answers he will be 'sussed out' i.e. he will be able to relate a lot of detail when he tells the story but is unable to answer the questions as clearly – it is *incongruent.*

They may over stare at you especially after they have lied. It's a bluff. They are working very hard at trying to be the poker player.

"Don't you dare challenge me!" Is what they are trying to convey.

Alternatively, they may struggle to hold your gaze at all. They don't want you looking into them. Most probably they will look down, shamefully.

Note the forced exaggerated smile after they've spoken. Trying to make what they have said palatable and not give anything away, also challenging you not to challenge them with anything like suspicion which would be deemed unpleasant and upsetting. Similarly, look for a very small smile that may dart across their lips after they have lied; an almost uncontrollable flinch. It's hard to spot, but it says that they think they have been smart by getting away with a lie.

I watched a documentary about Isobel dos Santos the wealthiest woman in Africa who is accused of exploiting her native country Angola. In two interviews she regularly let small smiles flash on her face after answers to questions about her business dealings that netted her masses of money. I know that police detectives will replay film of suspects telling their story frame by frame in order to spot this 'tell'. I learnt this one from a programme about investigating murders. The frozen frame of a flicker of a smile on the face of a mother who had murdered her children caused the detectives to pursue a conviction.

Listen to the tone of their voice. Check it against the tone when it was obvious they are telling the truth: telling you about stuff that they have no need to lie about. Typically the pitch goes up when they lie.

Another one to look out for is an incongruence of action and words.
'Do you know the whereabouts of the body of Peter Falconio?' (or a question to that effect).
Joanne Lees: 'No,' whilst nodding yes.

49

It's almost imperceptible. Again, police will freeze frame video to look for it. So if you try it have it planned out. Have the question ready and be focusing intently on the person. The truth leaks out.

If you want to influence your target then you have to understand them. You have to understand them as a person. You need to know what is important to them and what they want and where they are up to each time you meet them. This is going to take questions and you need to know if they are telling the truth.

And so how do you lie to them?

Well my Libertine you've got to learn to keep things simple. Stay with the open body stance or position with hands in full view, and stay still. A half toothless smile, a nod, an eye meet. You maybe wanting to squirm and twist. You need to redirect these urges. Do something that no one can see. How about pushing your toes into the ground in a pulsing like fashion? Or, keep squeezing and releasing your anal sphincter?

And read the above and do the opposite, perhaps..!?

'No your honour, I've never forged a signature in my life.'

Chapter 5
Rapport & Snake Oil

Or, how to get your teeth close to their neck!

Gaining rapport with your target is vital my Libertine. This is about 'being in tune'. The objective is to get the person feeling comfortable with you. If they feel comfortable with you they will like you. If they like you they will feel more at ease with sharing information with you and listening to and taking on board your ideas.

Remember: people by nature seek harmony and want approval.

It's going to be a whole lot easier to get someone to do what you want if they like you. Don't confuse this with *purely* getting them to like you; it's not the sole aim of the exercise. They may like you but this doesn't guarantee they'll do what you want. They may like you but respect and listen to someone else. And don't make it the 'you' show; you're not trying to prove you should be a celebrity. Influencing people is not about just being nice, or trying to be Mr. Charisma. In fact, effective influencers are often disliked by some as they often have the guts to deliver the home truths that others won't [more]; they are prepared, when appropriate, to be brutal with their target. You may resort to being brutal with a deluded prospect....or even shame your target away from deluded ideas.

If you quickly build rapport it will help when, soon after, you need to brutally qualify. This is the critical next step and needs couching, i.e. your prospect needs to be 'softened up' because qualification can, and often should, sting your prospect.

Keep in mind that what you are engaging in is rather like a chat with an agenda which you control. Always bear in mind how you use your time is critical.

Let's highlight a sequence here so that you have a plan. Firstly, when you connect with a target, try and create rapport. You maybe pre-armed with some questions about a current issue (keep it neutral) and ask them what they think about a subject; get them talking and listen, join in (which doesn't mean hi-jack their subject and make it about you). Or you may have a short story to tell them, and I mean short like absolutely no more than one minute. Maybe something that shows you as vulnerable (not a complete idiot); get their defences broken down. You come in peace. You are not a threat.

Social grease doesn't hurt. It's worth getting tooled up with some small talk. Read the papers, watch the news and make mental notes about what's happening. Keep the usual out of it, religion and politics. No need to express your opinion on anything, yours doesn't matter; it's about the client's. Don't go in gibbering. Don't feel compelled to fill the silence.

"Sooo, how's your day been?"
Small talk is a good weapon in terms of building rapport. Few are really good at it, but it can be learnt and practised. It never ceases to surprise me how people are happy to chat about trivia. Let's face it, it's what politics is all about; gossip, hearsay, and in theory it's politicians that have the most power in most countries. Remember: we are dealing with humans and so rationale and logic have little to do with decision making.

A recent survey found that patients perceived GP's (doctors) that were personable to have superior medical skills.

Charming small talkers go along way. They are liked and people make the assumption that what they say is important, and so people are more easily led by them. On a bigger scale great orators are the people who have led even though their logic and ideals were corrupt, e.g. A.Hitler. On a personal level, people who can chit chat make people feel comfortable and so they are, by default, *trusted,* and that is what this is all about.

Remember, however, the primary objective is : GET THEM TALKING. Take time out to practice if it doesn't come naturally. Have a chat with someone in a shop and agree with everything they say. What does it matter? Act like it's the first time you've ever heard whatever they're saying, alright calm down don't overdo the dramatics. Repeat things they say back to them. Ask them to expand on things. Hey, if you're not careful you might learn something.

Sometime ago I read about a telephone company that during it's research found one word was spoken more, by a large multiple, than any other.

The word?
"I".

Guess what? Other people are more interested in themselves than you, get over it: hence the success of social media. If people didn't have this huge drive to talk about and display themselves, social media wouldn't exist. It seems to me that self obsession is lorded and rewarded, but you can use this to your advantage. One female, especially, essentially made her and for her family fame and money from (and to me seems only capable of) taking pictures of herself!

Not so long back I picked up a thick expensive hardback book in a reputable bookstore. A book of madam's selfies. In the foreword it suggested that you the fan should be grateful for the effort involved as she (yeah really!) had sorted through 450,000 (I think I staggeringly recall) selfies to produce this book! Perhaps it should be heralded as the next guiding book of religion (Bible, Koran etc...hey, maybe its time to move on?)! You want inspiration as how to 'make it', then stop reading this nonsense and get that book – the high priestess of self absorption is now a billionaire! It's only a scam if you're not in on it!

So I urge you to imagine putting a ring though the other person's nose of self obsession and leading them.

"Oh, I see, so you're saying.....umm, how about that...you know, I never thought of it like that....what brought you to that conclusion?....that's an interesting way of looking at it, how did you come to that way of thinking?.....",
"..what do you think to?...how did you find that?...what made you do that?...how do feel about this?....". Most people are self absorbed and you'll find they don't need much provoking to tell you about them or their opinions. There's a well qualified philosopher in all of us; get through to it, learn something. Remember that line about walking a few miles in the other man's shoes?
Another observation of mine: people with money always have a desire to tell you how they got it. That is why a large portion of criminals give themselves away...
'..don't tell anyone but ....hey, aren't I smart...?!'

People love to tell you how 'clever' they are.

People that went to Oxford or Cambridge University always tell you so within ten minutes of meeting them: they are well practiced at smuggling it into the conversation.

So there's a cautionary moral here. I know you've been sharing that little room for most of the day for several months now but just think before you over share my Libertine, that confidante might not be all they seem either.

Know this: the person who can listen, truly listen, is a very rare individual. Being able to listen is a very powerful tool. Also, people crave to be listened to. It stems from childhood. We crave the attention of other people that listen to us. It looks and feels like they care. If they believe you care then you must be *trust worthy*.

When doing residential sales, for the fun and interest value I used to decide some days to find out as much as possible about people. I'd ignore the idea of selling anything almost completely. Try it, you'll learn loads and you'll find they eventually ask you to sell to them and what's more, they'll help you. They'll feel indebted to you if you have listened to them, and if you practise being patient and encouraging them [more] you'll be amazed at what they will tell you.

Guys: "..he never listens...". Without doubt one of my major weapons has been listening. Try it. Trust me. If you listen they will feel 'close' to you.

See how long you can keep people talking. After they've said something keep silent and nod, raise your eyebrows, maintain eye contact and they'll feel compelled to say more. They will feel compelled to fill the silence.

Don't be afraid of a pause; resist the temptation to fill the silence. The pause may feel painful but believe me they'll give you the real them; give you an insight to what they are thinking. The pause will put them under pressure to say more and the more will most likely be the bit they wanted to hide, the stuff behind the mask.

Also, and this is a great technique, try repeating the last phrase they just said back to them and then stay silent. They'll be compelled add more, qualify what they've said and tell you the truth. You want this extra bit. So rather than waiting for them to stop speaking so you can give your response, practice getting that extra bit. Just as you have a plan, a routine, so have they...you need to get passed it!

Remember: if they're talking and you are listening, you are influencing.

Understand: the person who is silent is thinking faster. Think about yourself when you've been listening. You have spare capacity to think about....implications of what they are saying. You can anticipate what they are going to say next, you can think about other things and you can observe them, pick up information. They, on the other hand, are stuck mentally trying to talk, express what they have to say. The person listening has the advantage and remember, you have an agenda you're trying to influence them and so you want an advantage.

Target: "....blah,blah and then we went to an out of town car dealer and bought a red car."

Libertine: "bought a red car." Silence. No need to even lift the tone to make it a question.

T: "Yes, well, err." They weren't going to add to it but they'll search around for something to say, often the truth because it'll come to their mind more easily...

"Frankly, it's not my favourite colour but my wife insisted."

L: "wife insisted", silence plus toothless smile and nod.

T: "..well err, when I say insisted, I suppose in truth it had low profile tyre which I wanted so I compromised on the colour."

L: "..on the colour..."

And so on. You'll be amazed what people will tell you. If you're into getting gossip from people this works a treat!

I think this is a technique that counsellors use. Two parallel professions, i.e. about communication. I call it the squeeze *trick*.

You're trying to get inside their head find out what they're really thinking and remember, your target will have a 'patter' too which you have to get past rather than accept. This technique of repeating back to the prospect is great for objection handling too; it's a personal favourite of mine [more].

Have time for people. What they say is important. More important than what you say - get over it.

Don't confuse listening with waiting to say something. I knew a salesperson like this, he'd hum whilst the prospect was talking and would take gulps of air whilst lifting his head ready to interject with what he had to say because it was much more important. He'd masterfully chip the end off a prospect's sentence, put them right probably with something of a contradiction, humble them a bit, pick them up on a couple of points that they obviously didn't fully understand. He knew best for goodness sake. He'd had a lot of jobs.

Think of it this way - you are demonstrating that you have respect for this person as a fellow human being. Life isn't always easy and here's this person battling through. You don't know what they've been through, what they're going through in life. We've all had difficulties, problems with our upbringing, problems with families, illnesses, deaths, joys. Give some empathy. Show some respect. They're not just a bland prospect; they are an individual with lessons to give.

You think you know a lot? Well you don't. You don't know much. Of all the stuff there is to know you only know a particle (no matter who you are). Been to a reference library, done searches on the internet? And that's of the stuff we know we know. What about the stuff we recognise we don't know about e.g. what's in our Oceans, outer space, and then further the stuff we don't know we don't know. You know virtually nothing, like everybody else. This is reassuring. Bear this in mind when you manipulate: nobody is going to intimidate you: you don't know much but neither do they!

So, if you keep quiet, this person might teach you something. Funny thing, if you listen to them they might return the compliment and they might be ready to learn from you. So, make it a sharing thing. You can make your agenda the platform from which you can really connect with people. Your agenda can form stepping stones to a connection with other people.

Buuuuut .....don't be a dustbin for other people's junk. A lot of folk lack self awareness and when they get talking they won't stop and will happily make a victim out of you.

Especially males over 50. Read on and learn how to interrupt and steer them.

Trade with your prospect: give and take.

Here's an extension of the squeeze *trick*.

"...so let me get this straight, what you're saying is..." and then say it a bit wrong back to them and let them put you right. They'll feel as though they have really connected with you. They will be at pains to explain to you. They will be pleased with themselves when they see that you grasp, second time around, what they are saying. They will want to protect you. They will be less intimidated by you because they will feel that you are not smarter than them and so they will let their guard down, and so let you put your cloak around them my Libertine! Appearing a bit daft or naive is very useful, much better than being a smart ass.

A chap down the road from me walks a bit pigeon toed, wears scruffy teddy bear like jumpers and ill fitting cord trousers his hair is scruffy with thick glasses on the end of his nose, and he sports the permanent toothless grin of the village idiot. When you talk to him he lets you spend a while explaining who you are in an animated fashion because he claims he's got you confused with some one else. He is a self made multi millionaire and is as shrewd as a snake. No need to show your hand. I'm pretty sure it's an act which buys him time when he's pressed about something he's supposed to know or admit to.

I have a friend who has made a lot of money and I have studied him. One of his primary skills is his ability to listen. He always knows exactly what is going on in his environment, in the community, who's buying what, who is sleeping with who, because he *listens* to people. And people know he listens and so they want to visit him and tell him things.

Never be afraid to declare your lack of knowledge or that you don't understand. This makes you vulnerable, approachable and a human being and, in turn, it gives you charisma, real charisma. No one likes a 'know all'. It takes courage to admit you don't know everything or something, but people will quietly admire you for it. It will make you accessible.

I love that line in the film Margin Call when things (the 2007/8 crash) are about to go south: Jeremy Irons is the big cheese of this share dealing company and he's been asked to attend a meeting in the middle of the night (he arrives by helicopter) and a team have to break the news of impending disaster.

'Just explain it to me like you would a seven year old..it's not intelligence that got me to where I am..', ahh, but right there contrarily, it was...not academic intelligence maybe!

Another *trick* my Libertine is to *politely* disagree for the sake of digging in to them.

"Oh, I didn't realise that, but I thought the opposite was true...that, blah, blah, *something contradictory..*".

You push against someone 9 times out of 10 they'll push back: put you right / defend their position. They'll get a bit worked up. This is good. Chemicals will start to run through their body. The exchange with you will have gravity because it has heightened emotions associated with it.

Maybe prod them a bit more.. "nooo, nooo, come on, seriously...you don't truly think...how did you come to that conclusion...can't be true...", etc.

Then start to swing around to their way of thinking.

"...what? Hold on, so you're saying....what, do you think I've got this wrong...you know what I need to rethink this one....hey, I'm beginning to think your right"

And then...

"oh I get it....wow, I've been wrong all this time..", few people admit they are wrong and this will be quietly admired...

Either way, let them 'win', bring you round and educate you. Likelihood is: when it comes to the real agenda, i.e. presenting your good idea, they're more likely to come round to your way of thinking. They like that you've made a concession and they will return the gesture, and you've taught them that it is okay to concede and agree. You're trading.

Get to appreciate people and they will automatically appreciate you.

And now: on to flattery, you gorgeous, brilliant creature you.

The use of flattery can be part of that grease. Use carefully. Its application is an art. Practice on friends etc. Do not flatter the person/persona or anything personal, clothes, height, etc. Why not? It is 1. Too obvious. 2. Can make people feel uncomfortable / self conscious. 3. The feature you flatter may be giving them a complex, inwardly they will not agree with you and will be disturbed by the fact you bought it up 4. Can be perceived as condescending.

Essentially, to offer a compliment about someone's appearance is personal and judgemental – so keep away. Unless it's a female who has obviously made an effort for a date..'Hey...you look great..'

Flatter what they do or have done instead. Don't be gushy and cheesy, they'll see you coming and then from the beginning you're dead.

"..goodness, that's a lot of responsibility….."
"…that's a lot of complexities to deal with…."
….hmmm, got to be able to handle a lot of pressure…"
"….I guess it's an ability to manage several things a once….."
"..that takes a lot of stamina….."
"……helps develop one's patience, that one…."
"….have to be fresh and alert all the time…."
"...you've done well to create all this…."
"...you must have a great eye for detail..."
"...that must take a lot of forward planning…."

Walk in their shoes. Have a look around you and get a feeling for what other people have to go through on a daily basis. Recognise their talents. Why not? It'll make you both feel good. They'll like having you around. Make being with you a positive experience and that means making the client feel good about them. To make them feel good, make them feel valued.

You'll be amazed how just a smidgen of flattery will go a long way. We all crave it. Its how people with charm get along and charm goes along way. I can write a short list of people who have flattered me and I will forgive them anything.

Two people have jumped into my mind. One is an old mate called Dino.

He had loads of friends, everybody liked Dino. His catch phrase, "Yeah Greg, I'm like you", or similar "Yeah, I'm like that", "Yes Greg, know what you mean, I feel like that." It wasn't just me, he did it to everyone, slut. Take it from me, Dino is like you, you'd like him! He'd often append it with a touch of his hand on your arm say....NLP...another friend of mine, a real killer sales person, Gordon; Mr McCharm himself, he was the master of this move. It's called an anchor [more].

It's hard not to like someone like that... [*mirroring*]. Appropriately tactile and always so glad to see you, like a dog, unconditional, clear of agenda and judgement.

Please note my Libertine...*may I suggest* that a person's name is the most important word to them ever......get it right....Exercise: try and use the other person's name in a meeting/phone conversation – 3 times, and 3 times only. Always say their name at the beginning or in the middle of a sentence, not at the end. At the beginning of a sentence means friendly, at the end it's a command. Check their name at the beginning of the conversation; repeat it back to them, maybe in a soft pleasant tone, like it's your baby's or that of a loved one. Make sure you've got it right at the beginning. If you're speaking to them on the phone and you are able, write it down there and then, i.e. the name they like to use. It's not uncommon in the heat of an intense telephone conversation, especially, when you are concentrating on what you are saying and what is being said to go and use the wrong name. I can't say exactly why this is it just happens and completely undoes all the progress you made. It sounds disingenuous. I know I've done it several times. I put the phone down after the call having used the wrong name and cringed for an age. Write their name down in bold in front of you if circumstances allow...or even say their name out loud a few times before you make the call.

Rapport: this is the key to softening up your victim my Libertine. You can't just go in and sink your teeth into their neck; you've got to charm them first. I believe that charm can be learnt and it goes along way. Charm can be deadly. It is my belief that females are the stronger sex. They are more resilient. They work better together. It is proven that they are better liars and lie earlier in life. They are emotionally more mature (generally); able to multi task better, better communicators and collaborators. But they are suckers for charm. And a great way of being charming is to listen and agree, but with that, to be supportive.

'..the devil will return as a good looking charming man..'

Never judge what people say unless your judgement is positive and therefore reinforces something about them or something they have said.

Also, try and remember things about people and refer back to these things at a later date. Especially stuff they are either worried about or things they are trying to achieve.

'....did your wealthy grandma's persistent cough get better..?'
'...how did you get on signing up that lucrative business deal with all that commission?'

Referring back to stuff of concern or interest to them will connect them to you.

"....oh yes, Ms Libertine is such a caring, genuine person...I think that changing my will is a good idea."

Chapter 6
Speaking in Code

I'll summarise. Rapport is about walking in their shoes, having empathy for the other person. To get this both parties need to be communicating. You need to be using their code. You need to decipher their code and use it. Speak their code.

You'll stand more chance of influencing someone if they understand you. To enhance the chances of them understanding you: you need to speak their language.

Use the same language as them. Use the same words as them. Use the same phrases as them. Deliver phrases they use the same way and the same speed, the same pitch and the same volume. I will even gently change my accent. Mimic them. Tread carefully, I didn't say mock them.

Think through that last small paragraph. You master this and you'll get your way.

Like the mirroring of their actions and body language you are also going to mirror what they say. If they hear themselves in you then guess what? They will feel *safe* with you. They will listen to you. They will more easily accept what you are saying. Remember that it is easy to think that the other person is a centred confident being, but often they are not. They are very possibly riddled with anxiety and crave reassurance. Enter you my cloaked Libertine, stage left.

I watched a documentary on Michael Hutchence the rock star the other day. Quite obviously he had 'it' in spades. Simply a beautiful man and would be the envy of all others; successful doing what he enjoyed, wealthy, talented....blah, bloody, blah .....and of course, had she had the chance my wife would have traded me in too! But I was surprised (and somewhat reassured) to learn that he was riddled with angst.

Proponents of NLP (neuro linguistic programming) science claim we can be divided into three groups; Visuals (majority), Auditory (minority), Kinaesthetic (the rest). I'm not so sure it's that simple, i.e. that we fit directly into one of the three categories, but it's fair to say that one of the three will prove to be the dominant driver for most of us.

The basic concept is that one of the above dictates the way we experience life. Visuals *as you would imagine* [a great line for binding people in....Prof Warrick... more?!] think visually, i.e. paint pictures, play video/see pictures in their minds.

An auditory person's thoughts are dominated by sounds; accordingly, they make good musicians. I'm definitely not one of these having just learnt to play 'happy birthday' after playing the sax for 30 years, but I've met some that can listen to a tune and immediately replicate it. I remember it's said that these types tend to be indecisive, how true that is....?

A kinaesthetic experiences life predominantly through feeling, they are more sensory and it is said they tend to make better athletes. They are more in tune with the way they feel and are therefore more in tune with their physicality. Feelings make themselves 'felt' in the body.

Kinaesthetics are able to listen and tune into feelings that are held and expressed in the body. *I am currently in a programme of stretching out a ball of tightness in my shoulder that has plagued me all my life. It is congealed, unexpressed emotion created by CPTSD (complex post traumatic stress disorder) from my childhood. As the area of tightness slowly releases I feel the fear and shame (that was projected on to me) expulse. I am a proud member of a group of male survivors of CSA (childhood sexual abuse) and I am not alone in the understanding that trauma, and therefore effectively unexpressed emotion, is held in the body; in the muscles and it works its way into the fascia. It won't be long before the association between trauma treatment and physiology becomes widely appreciated among the medical profession as a primary route to recovery and mental health – rather than just issuing chemicals.*

This relates to us my Libertine because we can pick which they are and adjust our language, tone and behaviour accordingly.

We pick them by watching their eye movements. Visuals look up to the sides or gaze at the middle distance when they are thinking and recalling information. They are seeing things in their mind. An auditory will look to the sides, almost as if they are listening for the information, level with their own eye line. A kinaesthetic will look down in an attempt to feel the experience. Again, like they are looking into their body trying to feel how they felt or how information is affecting them physically and emotionally.

It's interesting to experiment with this. How entirely accurate it is, I'm not sure, your call given that I've heard/read that people use all three but have a dominant trait. So your call, but I have noticed patterns that fit the theory. I would say that it has value but is imprecise.

Trick....
Ask your target something about their past.
'What did you do last weekend?' and then watch their eyes. Up, to the side or down?

It may take a couple of goes to be sure: separating out the kinaesthetic is quite easy but separating an auditory from a visual is a little more difficult. But remember that it is believed there are considerably fewer auditory people than the most common of the three which are visual.

So let's start with the visual. You ask them what they did last week and they'll try and re-run a movie or a bunch of still images in their minds. They will look up and to their left. They are looking into the past, searching the film archives. So to influence a visual you need to select visual words.

"...how does that *look* to you..?"
"..let's take a *view* on this..'
"...Can you *see* yourself getting involved...?
"...the *picture* is *looking* a lot *brighter*...'
"..when you say it like that the *vision* becomes a lot *clearer*.."
"....yes, I *envisage* a situation that *de-mists* the problem..."

There are many for the visuals. It's most probable that your target will litter their dialogue with visual words, which you should reflect back to them.

Another thing about visuals is that they will probably speak the fastest of the three. It's likely that the visual will become impatient if you speak slowly and you will lose them; their minds will drift and they will associate you with irritation. Not what you want.

Given the 'last weekend question' the auditory will look to their left side. They are actually trying to replay the weekend in sounds, i.e. the sounds and conversations they heard.

So again, with an auditory it is words based around sound that will de-code them.

"...can you *hear* what I'm trying to say.."

".how does that *sound* to you?

"..does that *ring* a *bell*?"

"...there's a *harmony* about it, don't you think?..'

"..lets work in *chorus* together..'

"..that's right, you start to get *in tune* with the whole idea.."

"..of course, *trumpet* the positives…"

An auditory may well be susceptible to a pleasant voice tone, soft, easy. They won't be so concerned about what you say, more about how you say it. Beware; they will be very susceptible to any irritation in your voice. Take your time with an auditory. Don't gibber at them quickly. They won't be listening to what you say but more the way you say it. Be seductive and when necessary be clear and firm.

Lastly: the kinaesthetic. Their heart rules their head. They make decisions primarily on how they feel about stuff. So you are going to make them feel good.

There don't seem to be so many trigger words for 'kino's' but they have a particular weakness [more].

'..so tell me, how do you *feel* about the idea..'

'…it's a great *sensation* to be a part of it...'

'…lets get in *touch* with the whole experience..'

'…when you get *closer* to ownership you'll *feel* good about it…'

'…once you've jumped you'll feel more *relaxed*..'

'…a *sense* of *calm* will envelop you once you've made the right decision.."

"..there's a *warmth* about the thought isn't there…"

A kinaesthetic will most likely speak the slowest. Evoking their feelings takes time. It's almost as if there is a lag time between them bringing up their feelings, recognising them and then converting them; they must re-evoke their feelings and then interpret them into words. When watching a documentary notice the way victims talk about a past incident that had a profound effect on them. It takes time for them to express themselves. Similarly, you must be patient with a 'kino'. If you are not, e.g. you interrupt them, they will shrivel away from you and hold back on making a decision, plus they will block you in the future. And always pause between them finishing speaking and you speaking. Why? Because they expect you to be absorbing what they are saying and converting it into your feelings. If you don't they won't take what you say seriously.

That's why a lot of athletes don't interview very well. In TV everyone speaks quickly and on cue, i.e. there are no pauses until they have to interview an athlete.

How do you feel when people use phrases that you aren't familiar with? Annoyed? Typically you don't want to ask them what they mean; no one wants to look foolish. So if you use lingo on a client, in an attempt to make yourself look smart, guess what? They don't understand you; people are less likely to accept something they don't understand, and you've probably annoyed them into the bargain. People don't get positively influenced by people that annoy them.

Using 'lingo' doesn't convince people. Blinding people with nonsense and baffling them may be a way of spinning them around. It's the conman's route. You might chose to use TLA' (three letter acronyms) and/or 'in' phrases or terminology related to the concept you are getting the target to own…but, it's a risk.

More often than not the client won't ask you what they mean. People don't like to look foolish and it takes someone that is very self assured to stop you and ask what something you've said means. They stay silent. If you practice you can see a stunned like look go across their face if they hear something they don't understand. It reverberates in their mind. It doesn't process through and slows up the absorption of the words that follow whilst they wrestle with it and try and make sense of it. They are no longer totally tuned into what you are saying. If they don't stop you they either; leave it and skip to what you are saying and therefore leave a blind spot, or they drift away and start to rely more on the tone of what you are saying in order to stay with you. The effect is rather like the sensation of being spun around. It disorientates them.

I knew a chap who held a very high position within a global advertising agency who was a master at this. I went on several 'calls' with him. I was amazed at the amount of bullsh@t he came out with and the people he was serving it to were successful business people, shrewd as you like.

We nicknamed him Professor Warrick. He wore an ill-fitting suit, his hair was dishevelled with big glasses on the end of his nose and he always carried an old leather briefcase stuffed full of papers which he never opened. It was an image that was incongruent with his environment given he was supposed to be wearing a sharp suit and look sharp. I watched him clumsily hand out documents, after rummaging around, that meant nothing with graphs of nonsense on. People assumed that he knew what he was talking about. He was non-threatening because his persona was that of an academic rather than a rival. He sounded smart because he spoke with *certainty*. The effect was to give an air of superior knowledge. It was though he didn't condone the behaviour of those around him, he didn't try to fit in and he didn't have to: he was separate, but there to help. The directness and certainty in his voice coupled with this academic image gave an air of someone that had looked at the situation from another viewpoint. Although the academic imagery was suspiciously viewed in the business arena it was also quietly respected or, at least, was considered wise to listen to. And the businessmen didn't want to look daft. They didn't want to give an academic the opportunity to be in any way condescending about their own territory. So they never questioned anything he said, although, to be fair, the meetings were always framed [more].

I was always amazed at that the way these shrewd business people never questioned him. His certainty mixed with this look of vulnerability, of not trying to compete, was part of his guise and it worked a treat – he mesmerised them.

The other part of his act boiled down to just a few phrases which he delivered with aplomb.

Just before he was about to pour a bucket of bulls@t over them...

"…and of course, it's *as you would expect*..the blah, blah, blah…"

"…*I don't need to tell you* what's going on here, you'd see that, blah, blah, blah.."

"…*it's nothing new*, so when I say blah, blah…"

"…*you already understand* that….blah, blah…"

So in effect, the next bit of what he was about to say was pre-alloyed against being questioned. He programmed their minds to accept what he was going to say. When he went on to deliver the totally unqualified 'great' news that they didn't quite understand, in their minds they would be re-assuring themselves.

So now they are baffled, they don't understand what he is talking about which is because what he was saying was incomprehensible nonsense. But the self talk in their minds would go along these lines…

"..oh, I needn't worry it's 'as I would expect'..I've heard this before, I already understand this it's just that I don't at the moment, but I'd better not say because I don't want to look like an idiot.."

People never stopped him and declared that they had no idea what he was talking about. They wouldn't admit it. What's more, what he had to say was positioned in a way that told the prospect that they already understood what he was saying and that made it even more difficult to declare their ignorance. No one likes to look like an ignorant fool. If they didn't understand what he was saying they felt as though they should and that it was their fault that they didn't. That they were the fraud rather than him!

But Professor Warrick was a con man, my Libertine. Naughty, naughty boy that Professor Warrick.

But coming out with stuff that the client doesn't understand can work against you.

Ever been 'sold' at by the technical whizz?

He'd assumed the client had an amount of knowledge, but had successfully demonstrated that the client didn't know that much by using terminology known only to those in the know, like him. He'd successfully humbled the client and expressed his superior knowledge. Was the prospect convinced?

Actually, the client had humoured him. She listened to what he had to say, although she glazed over occasionally. Fairly early on she had 'tipped away' and decided to put on a mask. She had refrained from shouting her questions over the top of his 'pitch'. She extracted some relevant information from him and when he'd finished she politely told him that she would need 'some time to think about it'. Quietly, she had decided, given that she didn't fully understand what had been said, that she needed to do more investigation. She was in a meeting mostly when he called back. Had he convinced her? It was a dreary presentation, like listening to a lengthy radio broadcast that frequently went out of tune.

Use language that matches your target's culture – without condescension.

Be wary of lingo. If you use it expand on it. They may have already heard some lingo related to this idea so expand it into layman's terms, inwardly they'll thank you for it and it will boost your credibility.

"Model beta x has the inverter processor, which someone explained it to me as being the bit that pops up and warns you if it's getting too hot. Forgive me if I'm using too simplistic terms; also, please speak out if I say something that's a bit weird, this industry is soaked in lingo and technical stuff. Yes?" pause, nod, raise eyebrows, look innocent/a bit daft (simpletons toothless smile)/approachable. It's ok to ask/it's ok to seem daft.

You're going to break it down so we all understand it. Don't be afraid of seeming a bit dumb, it beats trying to look smart. In fact, you'll look more confident and it will boost your credibility. Remember, in the big scheme of things, you know Jack all. You're not there to intimidate them.

If they've interpreted something you said into their own language repeat phrases/words they've used back to them. DON'T correct them. DON'T swap their words for yours. If they reinterpret your words to theirs, they are taking ownership, they are tipping over! Now they are buying into your idea. They understand it and what's more, they're looking for your approval. We all want approval. They are talking themselves into your idea...lovely..!

'...that's it... you've got it...I like that phrase...I'm going to use that next time..." "bung it in the thingo"...yes, yes I like that..'

If they use lingo that is specific to them/their trade etc, ask them to explain it (unless of course it's really is something you should know). Again, you'll learn something.

Trick : Let your target think they are smarter than you. They'll like you for it, but the fact is, you're leading them all the time my Libertine – ring through the bulls' nose.

Another *trick*: interrupting.

By the way...do you like being interrupted? Who does? But sometimes.. 'oh they do go on...'. The target may be drifting as they waffle on, drifting away from the matter in hand, drifting away from what you know will be good for them, in which case consider it a duty my Libertine, to bring them back in line with your thinking.

Try this one: someone is blithering on...listen carefully to the words, again like running alongside a roundabout, and then jump in and repeat the last phrase they just came out with and immediately change the subject by asking them another question...it'll stun them and they will answer it. You must have the question prepared in your mind.

Drivelling target :"...yes and I was walking, well not really walking more *ambling when I saw*...."
Libertine: "*ambling when you saw* - did you get to read the agreement?"

It kind of splices their mind.

The interrupting technique takes practice. Try it. It's rather like talking over the top of them, which the other person will find offensive, but this way they don't feel a thing. It's like you hijack their train of thought and direct it to where you want to go.

So, jump in and repeat their last phrase and then simply direct their attention to something else.

Target : "...back in our day we used to catch the number 15 bus all the way to...'
Libertine: "..the number 15 bus all the way - this gives you a classical look....and.... forgive me, what were your credit card details again?".

This one takes practice but works a treat. Gives you control: enables you to gently pull on the nose ring.

Aikido is a style of combat that completely absorbs the other person's force and uses it against them. I'm talking about resisting the temptation to resist. I'm talking about moving aside, letting them own the territory and walking along side them.

When you walk into someone's territory you are now where they live and breathe what they do. If you think you're going to tell them what they should be doing on the basis you know more about their lives than them, it maybe a mistake. It may cause your prospect to get defensive.

Libertine: "....you'll, I'm sure, understand this stuff better than me, but what I'm trying to say is.....blah, blah...I'm not explaining this too well, *how would you put it?*"

Client : "Well what you're probably trying to say is....blah....". They're going your way. They're reinforcing it in their minds.

Libertine: "... oh yes, I like that, that's a more succinct way of putting it...so in that case the benefit would be if you were to invest the money now then your returns are going to be bigger in the long term... yes, I see, *makes sense doesn't it?* Anyway...", and move on.

Later... "it's *like you were saying earlier* Bob...and then go on to repeat their phrases back to them....you don't want me to be de-motivated by low pay...", they understand you, you understand them, it's flattering for them. By repeating what they say back to them they feel reinforced. They feel *approved* of. You are in tune. Harmonise. You are in the same key (music).

The code of influencing is largely about being positive. That is scaring them away from danger and offering safe higher ground to be enticed towards. You've got to be a cup half full person; feel lucky. You know things will turn out. People are naturally attracted to positive people. People pay money to be entertained by positive people. They don't pay to go and listen to people moan. And positivity is contagious. If you're positive people will want to be around you and they will seek your approval because they will want you to *allow* them to be with you. They will be on their best behaviour and be positive back to you, and a good way of them choosing to be positive is to agree with you. They want you to remain positive: they don't want to upset you.

I knew another great salesperson who, if there was any negativity from his clients especially in the early stages of engagement, would always jump on it with theatrical hurt mixed with defensive anger. People don't naturally seek conflict, in fact the opposite, they want harmony and they don't like upsetting others. His overreaction would set them aback; startle them. But they would always retract and be apologetic almost like they had crossed a social taboo, said something they shouldn't have. At the same time they had been conditioned to be positive about my friend's suggestions going forward. They wouldn't want to risk upsetting him again.

Positivity is reflected in your language, in the words you use. Each word has a resonance; I believe it's something to do with semiotics which I understand to be about how a word is interpreted and how it is perceived. Never mind the complexities. Point is: there are a whole load of positive words and a whole load of negative ones.

Your dialogue should be loaded with positive words and phrases. Although perhaps not quite speaking like an excited children's TV presenter.

'...that's going to create a smooth handover....'
'....it's easy to control; the whole process is simple to do...'
'...it gets better the more you use it..'
'...the whole environment becomes a great platform for you to generate the space you need..'
'...it slides forward seamlessly to give you the advantage you want...'
'...a surprising bonus, it creates an energy I think you'll enjoy..'
'..your funeral will be the grand affair that a man of your great standing deserves.'
'..must say I am impressed the way you confidently grasped this wonderful investment..'

Practice littering your dialogue with positives. People will naturally devolve towards you. Each of us has an 'openness' you want to tap into. Similarly, each of us possesses a cynic inside: don't evoke this in other people, if you reflect cynicism, people will objectify you with negativity and will subsequently shut down to you, i.e. put in place barriers and block you.

Always be positive. Lead them to the light. You know what's good for them my Libertine; it's your duty to help those lost souls.

Here's one of the most important phrases I ever read about communication.

One match can burn down a forest.

"It's not your baby."

"I don't love you anymore."
"Well you are a bit fat."
"It's inoperable."
"I'm afraid the test is positive."
"you stupid child"
"it's a bit small."
"I've been declared bankrupt."
"It's got a tear in it."

Especially when offering a complex solution which may take several interactions. You may go to a lot of trouble, building rapport, getting to know them, several visits, done a lot of homework, expended a lot of energy etc.

"..well the updates don't work." A line my 'sales support' person came out with at a presentation to a group of senior employees from a blue chip organisation who after several visits, meetings, calls, proposals etc, etc, regarding the 'investment' in a considerable computer software and hardware solution that would have led to a lot of further opportunities with related companies....dead. I nearly stabbed him in the throat with my pen!

Think before you speak - every time.

Remember, they are interested in what you have to say. Phrases and words you use will resonate with them afterwards. Believe me; they will even use the words and phrases you use when you've gone. You are programming their mind more than you may realise. As a Libertine, get this, a prospect that is serious about doing what you suggest actually projects authority on to you, they give you authority, they want to, it makes them safe in doing so and therefore what you say is important, especially when they get close to agreeing with you. They will even recall a lot things you said early on, so think about what you're saying from the get go. Also, if they start repeating your phrases back to you – they've bought your idea, they are passing the tipping point [more].

There was a gentleman that had a successful chain of retail outlets in the UK sometime ago. I watched a documentary about him. He built the business up from scratch. He was a hero of society to my mind; the type that is essential. It would be hard to imagine the pain, dedication, hard work, sleepless lights, the worry, the physical and emotional strain he had been through to realise his vision.

One day he stood up in front of a large audience and gave a speech. They interviewed a journalist as part of the documentary who had obtained a transcript of the speech before it was presented. The journalist said, with glee, how this one line jumped out at him. Clearly, the kind of person lacking the kahoonas to do something constructive with his own life and, as such, could only undermine others. The journalist was poised so the moment it was spoken, the line was broadcast/published in the media.

The line went something like this "...I was asked by a customer how I managed to sell the products so cheap, and I said because the materials/quality are cheap...", or words to that effect.

Bang. It killed the business. 'One match...'...Apparently, the next day people were queuing to take their goods back. No one bought anything from his chain anymore. I think he went bankrupt. Clearly, what he meant was that the stuff was cheap because, ultimately, whilst a perfectly good product for the price, it wasn't top quality because the customer wasn't paying top price.

After that he was, to my mind, chronically and unfairly vilified. I heard a rumour he's back out there doing stuff. That takes strength of character.

I worked for a very, very astute Frenchman in Kuwait called Henri. He was a self made multi millionaire. He had stowed away on a ship when he was fifteen and arrived in the middle-east. He'd taught himself to read and write in Arabic and had a successful business. On his desk in his office in a prominent position he had a rectangular stand with a white piece of paper in it and on it was the word 'THINK'.

What you say is likely to be more powerful than you realise.

Trick: Parroting.
The other person that sprang to mind wanted me to get involved in a business venture. I nearly did until I found he'd been recently released after serving five years for fraud. I tried to think about how he'd gained my confidence. He was easy to be with. He listened intently to what I had to say; without cheesey smiles etc, he agreed with everything I said even when I went back and contradicted myself, like he was going through the journey in my mind with me (read that last bit again). Powerfully, he would 'parrot' things I had said previously; as though, in the interim, he had really thought about what I had been saying.

"..it's like you were saying before Greg, the whole…."

Here's one, "….I recall you saying, Greg about blah, blah, which got me thinking and perhaps it might be worth considering…..".

This demonstrates that you have been listening and, more, you've thought about what they said: can't get much more flattering than that. People like to be around people that make them feel good about themselves. That's you my Libertine. Parroting is a very powerful way of flattering someone.

The prospect is then ready to adopt your viewpoint and, if necessary, accept a new one (trade). You've softened them up. They may start with a, 'I'm not going to get 'sold' to' attitude and therefore maybe wearing a protective shell. You are going to melt it away.

You're like them. They're like you. What...you're convincing a human aren't you?

And the key is this: if they can relate to you because you related to them, they'll feel comfortable with you and......they'll TRUST you, and therefore feel SAFE.

It's not necessarily what you say; it's how you say it. I got invited to be in a short film. We agreed that there were a million and one ways to deliver the lines. Any one word can be delivered with any one of a myriad of inflections that will change its effect.

Speed and tone of speech is very important. The secret is to match the prospect. I've done a lot of selling on the phone, particularly getting appointments (when you were allowed to). I was the master at it. From the outset I used to match the speed and tone of the person I was speaking to. Not necessarily exactly, but certainly not the opposite. If they are quiet, be quiet, if they are softly spoken, ditto. Are they gruff? Speak quickly? Use short sentences? Are posh? Down to earth? Mimick them. A bit. When you have built some rapport you can gently step up the enthusiasm if necessary. What I'm saying is that if they are a lacking in energy, step along side and then gradually lift your energy level and they will follow you and so begin to be infected by your energy. I think it is better to start where they are rather than overwhelm them with high voltage energy at the beginning of an interaction. This may push them further back into their shell.

If in doubt, speak slowly and clearly. People that speak this way are considered to have authority and are therefore credible and more easily believed.

When I am going to ask them to agree with me, or tell them something I want them to believe, I lower the tone of my voice, I slow down, I move a little closer and I purr the words at them. And nod.

I used to match their breathe patterns too! Whilst they were talking (and therefore I have the advantage) I am observing when they take a breath and do so at the same time. I am getting in tune. I get in the same rhythm of breathing as my target and then really gently slow the pace of the breathing down. Take slightly longer intakes. You will find that the target follows you and consequently they become more relaxed. I get them feeling more relaxed with me and therefore I become easier to be with. It's hard to do but it works. You will feel your target becoming more open. They will want to buy you that drink. Or come back to your room for a drink from the mini bar....

Oh by the way: please, please, please stop saying 'Eeerrrrr...'. It reflects; uncertainty, indecision, dishonesty, sloth, disengagement, pomposity, incompetence and is seriously irritating. How? If you are an 'eeerrrer' then try slowing down your speech and/or try pausing and between phrases and work on the urge to fill the space with an 'eerrr'. Give your mind time for manoeuvre: to catch up. Or, shut up.

'*Please forgive* me, *may* I ask you to repeat that..?' (buy time). BTW: There is no counter to hyper politeness except reciprocation.

Another *trick* to use which is very powerful is the way you say their name. Again, their name is the sweetest sound they know. It has a resonance that they are used to. It is ingrained in them. In fact, there is a documented school of thought that advocates that the resonance, the vibration of a persons' name, the sound it makes, actually affects the nature of the person. A name dictates personality type! Could be true! Why not? So, when you use their name use it with reverence and care. Say it softly with love. Don't snap out the sound. A half beat of a pause before and afterwards – frame it – make it a special important word.

What you say and how you say it is very important. But don't forget, what your target says is even more important so.....shhhh...let them come under the cloak my Libertine, they want to!

Chapter 7
Tuning in and Traction

Have you ever tried to jump on to a moving children's roundabout? The roundabout is not going to stop and wait for you to jump on. If you misfire it can have dire consequences – falling flat on your face after being spat off.

When you meet your next slave or phone them, especially, they have stuff going on in their head: the chattering voice, as we all have, and they may also be experiencing some sort of emotional state. It's really worth bearing in mind that both of these may well not have anything to do with you or what you want. Or rather, the target may not be thinking and feeling as you would like.

You need to get in tune with your target and then you need to neutralise them. You need to find where they are up to. You need to read what state they are in when you meet them and adjust your rapport building skills accordingly. What's more, you need to do this every time you meet them. Never just pick up where you left off, even if you feel like you are going right back to the beginning with them.

You need to be ready to put a buffer in between what is happening in their life right at the moment you meet them so that you can launch forwards into leading them to the Promised Land.

Tune your rapport accordingly when you first meet them. The first time you met them they may have seemed to have all the time in the World for a general chit chat. The next they may seem a bit gruff. Humans are moody creatures, we oscillate constantly. Don't go in or approach them with a prefixed agenda. You've got to be flexible. The idea is to get in step with them as quickly as possible.

Think of a time a friend who tends to talk a lot about themselves has called you up when you are busy. I have a friend, we go way back but our relationship has been reduced to rare telephone conversations and to be fair, when I see his name on my screen I wince. When he calls me it's because he's not busy. He always calls in the day. When he calls for some reason he always has a pre planned joke often about me worked out. And he speaks slowly. I, on the other hand, am horribly impatient and speak quickly and I'm always doing something in the day usually as quickly as I can. When he calls and I answer he immediately launches into some humourless monologue with his ears switched off. Even if I was only half busy and could have had a chat with him, by the time he has finished his spiel I want to shout down the phone and tell him to 'F off'. He never, ever, calls and asks straight away 'are you busy?', 'can you spare a minute for a quick chat?'. Which I could, but I don't. Because of his insensitivity to my situation I have spoken to him less and less over the years until now we just don't talk. It's a shame. A simple miscommunication regarding our communication has killed the relationship and somehow it would be really strange to actually highlight this issue so that we could get past it. That point has gone and now there is a cavern between us.

From the off, the conversation is about him. We need to reverse that thinking don't we my Libertine? It's not about you.

Read your target every time you meet them and be sensitive to the speed and amount of information they will share and can absorb, and measure the tone at which you can conduct your exchange.

A multi millionaire friend of mine who runs a busy business always responds to the question 'how are you?' when called on the phone with 'who are you, my doctor?' He is never interested in sharing pleasantries. Some insist on it and find it rude if you don't. It's often a cultural thing and can also be associated with the environment: the situation. I am the same as this friend. I happen to buy and sell properties and get called regularly by estate agents who give me their names but not always the agency and expect me to know exactly who they are, like I was waiting for them to call, and they ask me how I am. What do they care? It's disingenuous. A disingenuous start to the conversation: does that not set a precedent for the rest of the conversation?

I get loads of calls that follow this format.

'Hi is that Gregory?' (That's the name they have on the database. No one calls me Gregory).
'Who's this?' (gruff response + started I've to think 'what the f@k has it got to do with you whoever you are?')
'Hi Gregory (presumptive and now offensive) it's Paaffrrky from Symonndees n Barrkee' (incomprehensible but cheerful) 'How are you today?'

How about, 'well I am very busy but now you, whose name I missed / don't recall from a company whose name I missed / don't recall, who knows something about me which has made me suspicious, has just interrupted me to disingenuously ask me how I am as though they know me or care. So I was a little bit irritated by stuff before your call if you must know, but now I am ready to dump on someone and that person is you!'

'Goodness Gregory, what a bitter soul you are!'

Because *you* have appeared or called, just like the first friend I told you about, don't think that they should be grateful and therefore stop what they doing just to listen to you.

'Hey you lucky thing it's me, now...blah, blah. I'm going to tell you all about me...'

If the person is busy and gruff you don't need to be aggressive, but it's better to be succinct and clear. Their mind maybe racing and so it's preoccupied with all sorts of unrelated stuff, to cut through you need to keep it simple and clear. They will be grateful for this because what you are offering is an alternative to their current state of noise, i.e. a simple, easy to grasp clear pathway of thinking. You are calm, clear and concise and you sound sensible and not overly friendly.

'Hello my name is Mark, (trade – be open) is that Gregory?'

'Yes' (he gave me his name, I'll more than likely affirm mine but a bit gruffly).

'Sorry to interrupt you Gregory, I need to have a quick chat about [the issue], can I steal a minute please?'

Not - 'how are you today'.

The complete opposite may be true. They may be completely chilled and you are very busy but you need to talk to them and you want them to do something, or you need to get a point across, or want some information. They may want to chit chat but you may want to get straight to the point. Bad luck and good luck too, you're going to have to chit chat and listen, but whilst chit chatting, especially if you're listening, you're in control: you are leading them in. Let them go, let them chatter in fact, fuel it. Swallow your impatience.

So, you've gauged their mood and you have matched it. Let me be clear; if they're being aggressive or depressive don't completely mirror them, simply be empathetic. Adjust your tone so that it is complimentary to theirs rather than being discordant. There is the key word, 'discordant'. Think like you are a musician and they are already playing, what complimentary instrument would you play? What music and when so that you fall in harmony with them? But note: if their mood is negative, don't go there. Again, just be firm and clear; and if you like *a little* soothing…but watch the condescension. In essence, you want them to associate you with positive vibes. I'm not talking games show host which some people think you have to project, which can be off putting. I'm talking about always passing on a positive vibration and people will associate you with this.

I met a person; we'll call her Sheila, a 'professional' mental health patient. Sheila has had every therapy going. Her mental health is everybody else's responsibility (many share this attitude about their health: my friend is a nurse of 30 years, she'll testify). On her approach to a group talking they dissipate within minutes. Her 'vibe' is so heavy, slow, draining and self centred. What is your overall 'vibe'? Be aware of it. Be aware how you affect people. If they aren't talking as much as you don't kid yourself that it's because you are so interesting and that they have nothing to say. No, it's probably not. There is a lot of brutal honesty in this process, in your development as an influencer because it's going to take your full self awareness. If you are not fully self aware then you will not be aware of your prospect and therefore your ability to influence is weakened.

So you've tuned in. You've employed a couple of your rapport techniques. You've asked questions about them. You've helped them expand on stuff they have shared with you. This is the process of neutralising them. Separating them from what is going on and getting them ready to be receptive to the big idea that you have ready to plant in their minds......

"chit chat, chit chat [mostly them talking not you]...well anyway thank you for seeing me, so have you been looking long? Seen anything you like so far?"

The objective here is twofold. You are tuning into them as people at that moment. You are laying out the table all ready and fresh, ready for you all to sit down at the same time focused and ready to experience the same thing. It's likely that something else is going on for them just before you arrived that has little to do with you. You are looking to neutralise these thoughts with others that are simple and, as such, create a buffer between what they were concentrating on and what you want them to concentrate on.

If they start to rant on, don't just wait for them to finish so that you can launch into your story. Go with them, join in. Let them talk. However, you may want to employ the interruption technique to get them off talking about the cat's cough back on to explaining why they've been divorced four times: get them to expand on this...the four times divorced 'I keep marrying the wrong type..' concept. 'Oh it's not you then, it's the *type's* fault...' But remember, people find being listened to very flattering and makes them want to be around you. Truly listening is a learnt art: it is very difficult, not many people are very good at it. If you want to separate yourself from the crowd be a person that others want to be around. To be a person who can easily influence others, learn how to listen and practice, just like any other new skill you want to develop. It takes effort. Try leaving a pause after they've said something. Don't clip the end off other people's sentences as Sheila is apt to do by way of getting back to talking about her mental health issues and how 'they' are not doing anything about taking her problems away. Even if 'they' could they couldn't because she thwarts all attempts at help because if she were 'cured' the *safety* of her identity as mentally ill victim would be gone.

At some point you need to switch from the neutral dialogue to the important bit, i.e. getting them talking about and listening to the big idea. In the gruff aggressive greeting this will be quick but simple, and morsel sized.

You don't want them getting agitated by pouring loads of complex stuff onto them at the outset. You may have a pile of stuff you want to get through, i.e. concepts to explain, stuff you want them to understand, questions you want to ask but, again, remember you and your big idea is not 'the everything' that they have in their lives.

And if they don't seem happy when you are talking to them, i.e. something has upset them before your contact, you don't want to be asking them about their feelings towards your idea because they'll pin their bad mood onto it. Similarly, if they are waffling on you don't want to transmit impatience, but you do need to swing them onto the subject. This takes practice, and doing it seemingly with sincerity is something that takes skill. Again, practice with the interruption technique. Try it with your friends in a safe situation.

If you can't interrupt then listen and wait, then during a gap if possible, 'hmmm, that's interesting a bit like ...' and then into the subject.
'oh yes, I hear/see/understand/feel what you are saying, in some ways like that other thing we were chatting about. Did you manage to transfer the funds okay?'

When people are talking their minds are soaked up. If you are heard to accept what they are saying you aren't resisting them, and so they then won't resist you. Say something that implies that what they have just said is associated with what you want them to think about. Their minds will scramble for an instant trying to figure what that association is but it seems difficult to find one so they give up, it's too hard. If you follow with a simple question it is easier to stop trying to make the association that you seemingly saw but they didn't, and they just naturally answer your question. People's brains are lazy they follow the path of least resistance.

I call it the three tongued shuffle, it's a good technique to re-direct your target.

Target.. 'then the neighbour came round with some of those, now what are they, those dog biscuits?..'
Libertine:
1.[pause + thoughtful look] '...hmmm that's interesting...' [which acknowledges what they are saying but doesn't answer the question].

93

2. '...*similar to the other day* when we agreed on the investment for you...' [link phrase, then back onto the subject]

3. '...did you have anymore thoughts on the big idea?' [then the question which gets their mind working in the right direction].

They are now swerved on track. Trust me, they will instantly drop what they were saying (biscuits) without any discomfort.

Investigation.

The next part of the process is where you can get to the soft under belly of what they are thinking. Find out what they are looking for in life, where their buttons are which you are going to store up and press later: give them what they want to hear.

So rapport first....then...recap....where are they up to? Learn from them...what's changed...? What are their thoughts and feelings...?

Not the first meeting? You want them to have given your initial proposal some thought, even if it's negative. The worst case is if they haven't thought about it at all. If this is the case then you either, jolt them or drop them. A 'jolt' is to inflict urgency in a frank fashion. You may as well because it's the only hope you have of getting them to take your idea seriously. Say, getting committed to a relationship. You can't let this, 'not given it much thought attitude' continue. Either they are in or out. Don't kid yourself.

If they have been thinking about it, this is good. They have probably been chatting to someone about the big idea. They may probably have done some research. They may have gone a bit cold. They may have several questions. Equally, the idea may have grown in their minds and they may be hot for it and if this is the case then you need to tune into this and not hold them back.

Aside: I worked for a neurotic control freak selling a complex software product. Partly by luck and partly by going through the numbers I found a prospect that had done the investigation and had spoken to a couple of competitors in depth, and were on the edge of signing up when I met them. But the boss didn't like the idea that they hadn't gone through his perceived buying procedure and wouldn't let them buy! He pretty much told me not to bother with them!

"Oh, they're not buying it the right way!" I actually said this in a meeting.

Taking your idea on board such that your target owns it may not be a pre-set straight forward route.

Since you dropped the big idea on them chances are your prospect has taken the information you gave them and has since found out more, created questions/issues, plus they have drifted around with their thinking and feelings. Patience my Libertine, take in their situation – where they are at?

"...oh yes, I see, your priorities are.....you're keen to know about.... [give a list..]....well, *as is normal*, you need to know about... the product...the investment level...the returns...where we might live...putting mum in a home...selling the medals..., but forgive me, first let me tell you about the me/the company and how I/we've got to where I/we am/are so you'll feel comfortable about who you're dealing with, if that's okay?....." i.e. find out where they're at, and then swing them on to the track you want them on, which may mean going back to the beginning.

The point I'm trying to make is: you need to get in tune with the prospect, find out where they are up to. Are they aware of the service? Have they heard of your product? Have they used one before? Do they know anyone with one? How long have they been dating? Have they given the big idea much thought? Have they 'had the chance' to chat with their friends about you? What did they think? Have they met anyone they like in the past? Why did they like them? What happened?

You may have to back track them. Make sure they haven't skipped over something important in their thinking process.

Don't force a preconceived pattern of behaviour that you expect them to conform to; get in tune. Manipulation equals flexibility. Think: malleable.

You may be going back and meeting them again. Be sure; their lives have changed, they've had conversations, their attitudes and beliefs may have changed. You need to know where they're up to. Again, you will learn something and it may be that they've been chatting with the competition, i.e. someone that is offering something similar or may have expressed scepticism for you or your idea.

'..isn't it a bit quick to be thinking about letting them move in, you hardly know them...?'
'...well I don't think Dad will be keen to talk about releasing equity, he's not over mum's death yet..'

Don't start transmitting paranoia. Few people, or companies for that matter, are ideal from woe to go: have a perfect track record, or are morally perfect (would you want to end up like the last chap who was, two odd thousand years ago?). Your competition is no exception. Everybody has something they prefer to hide. Do not fret my Libertine, those doom merchants have fault a plenty. If some doubt has crept into the mind of your target, you need to know. You need to get it out, otherwise untended it will grow. Dig out that negative gossip and hearsay. Get them to air it. Often enough, once they do it will lose its hold on them.

'..has anything changed since we last met? [summarise previous agreements]...', again this is something few influencers do. How many real estate agents on seeing you again ask about your buying adventure since you last met?'

'..I bet your sister wasn't too excited about the idea of us living in your [deceased] parents' villa in Monaco....'

Between then and now things for you have changed and they have for the prospect too. You need to find out what. You are iteratively going back to the investigation phase: their attitudes, believes and desires/needs/wishes/knowledge will have changed. They will have spent time talking and thinking about the proposition and even if it cements what they thought last time, you need to know this. Especially if they have a partner or family member, or business associate you haven't met.

'Have you given our last chat much thought?'

'How have you been feeling about the idea we shared?'

'Did you get a chance to share the idea with anyone...what did they think...?'

Jump on to the revolving children's roundabout: get in step find out where they are at, and then you can reattach the leash.

This applies every time you speak to your next devotee. Think of the times you've gone around asking suppliers questions, generated their interest, got them sending info, calling you etc; you started out with an idea but it's changed in the meantime, and out of politeness you keep leading them on; you end up adjusting for them, leaving bits out, playing along with them. BUT they should be playing along with you.

You've better things to do than politely giving your target more information when what you don't know is that between the first meet and now is that...they've had a vasectomy... made another offer...been fired...split up...lost the lot at the casino....been diagnosed with a terminal illness....

And remember that you are asking them to make a decision and this is threatening, as such their thought patterns and emotions begin to exaggerate and are susceptible to irrationality. It's rather like dropping one of those soluble vitamin tablets into a still glass of water....you've made them fizz...!

So you're in tune and you've got them by the throat – albeit with a smile...the next phase....

Let's talk about traction; the down and dirty business of engaging your client. You're doing the ground work, stirring up the opportunities, looking for a bite.

Whoppee, you've got one. Whilst you're nurturing this bite and getting to know them and running around getting information and visiting them, and they're visiting you and so on, and you're developing quite a friendship and getting along nicely, you're influencing. No you're not, not necessarily. You may well be colluding to look like you're both achieving something. You may have entered into the buyer-seller quick step: you being nice to them and them being nice to you: a merry dance which ends in:-

'...well I enjoyed that, I must get back to my party, see you again sometime' / 'Let me think about it'...

With every scenario there is a script: a way of behaving and communicating. You need to adopt the script, get in tune and then break it. Get past the veneer.

So, always investigate. And then....

Get traction. *Get under their skin*. And moreover - **Qualify early on.**

Is this person going to commit? When are they going to buy? Have they got the authority? Have they been married before? Have they got any money? Have they bought before? When? Who from? How long have they been looking? What have they looked at? What did they like about her? What didn't they like about him? Are they prepared to make a decision? Do they need the consent of others? Are they working? Are their parents rich?........

In my opinion my Libertine, qualification is the key to success when it comes to influencing people. You, at least, need to be fishing in the right pond and similarly, you need to be turning on the charm for the right target. *You are worthy!*

You may well be able to sell ice to the Eskimos but why bother? It's going to be hard work and they probably haven't got a lot of money!

Don't waste your time, and don't let your target use you as a source of information. You do an important job; you are connecting people in the best way with your wonderful opportunity. You want to get them on board but you ain't no victim! Whilst you're with a timewaster you're not helping the person who wants to love you. Always presume from the outset that they might be a time waster.

So get the hot light out and get it focused on them......
it needs a bit of couching those buyer sensitivities an' all.

Before your routine, try and get them talking about their experience so far in terms of taking up your idea. If they volunteer any information about what they have seen, heard, feel, etc that is relevant to your proposition then this is GOLD. You need to feed on this but easy does it, you can easily turn them off. Appreciate they may have invested a lot of time and effort finding things out and may be a bit defensive about what they do and don't know.

Don't go out your way to agree or disagree with anything, even if they may have made the wrong assumption about something.

Where they are up to at that moment, i.e. their thoughts and belief, are what makes them 'them' at that moment, and you don't want to be passing judgement on specifics as they will feel you are judging them personally, not what you want. They own that information and if you are disparaging they feel as though you are criticising them as people and therefore, you're on thin ice. In fact, if you don't judge them they will open up to you more as time goes on.

"...it's quite a business this sorting through these kitchen/computer/dog training companies/investment schemes/love partners [get on their side of the fence, emphathise]...are you getting anywhere....?"

Use open ended questions, i.e. questions that cannot be answered with just a 'yes' or 'no'. The opposite type of question is called....?

"..has the [buying/dating] process changed your thinking from what you thought at the beginning to what you think/want now...?". A question like this will really open them up, get you *under their skin.*

Try and draw them out and listen. Get them to expand like we talked about earlier. At this point they will teach you how to convince them, if you'd just shut up and let them. Again, ask open ended questions, i.e. the ones that don't have a specific answer. Try and make them think a bit. And, value their opinion. People often attach to their opinions and belief with intensity. Some people go into public places wearing explosive vests and kill themselves and kill and maim innocent people because of their belief. Do not ever denigrate someone's opinion. Get into the habit of taking other peoples' opinions and beliefs very seriously. You don't have to agree with them, but don't argue with them either – well not if you want to influence them.

This first bit after the rapport is very important. As you get more experienced you learn to relax after the hello's and get them talking. This is where you will learn what to do and say to get that investment and you will learn other stuff too, about the competition, say. It might even be fun to defend your competition a little, suggest that they [competition] try hard at something or other; this builds your integrity and listening gives you more insight into your market. Treat them as researchers reporting back to you, you may be surprised at the misconceptions you've formed.

People gossiping about you?

You must jump on this one way or another, and quickly. Silence will add fuel to the negativity.

You have two options. 1. The angry denial. Shut it down. "How dare they?"

2. The brush off. It doesn't stick. "oh, they're probably feeling threatened".

But don't expand on it, i.e. don't ask for more detail about the gossip. The person reporting the gossip to you is likely to be a part of the negativity. They want a reaction and if you ask about it you are fuelling the whole episode.

Bear this in mind: they [your prospect] need your idea. Chances are they'd rather have it than not. They will therefore if they are serious, particularly educated ones i.e. they've done the leg work, tell you what they are looking for, i.e. what they've seen, liked and disliked. People want to impress and please. It's the child in all of us.

So, chit, chat, rapport and then gently swing into the influencing process...which is; get them talking about the process, what do they know, what have they assumed. DON'T ARGUE WITH THEM! They are not wrong. Just get in tune. Jump on the roundabout with them.

There are no set rules when influencing but there is a general pattern. Agreements of all types follow a general pattern. After you've built some rapport you need to get them talking as suggested, but what you want to find out is - their needs. What are they looking for? Where is their pain? What problems do they need to solve? Which areas do they need to improve? What pre-conceived ideas have they got? What are the necessities? What are the deal breakers/must haves?

Maybe you can do the needs analysis before your pitch, allowing you to tailor it, giving you an advantage. Maybe you trade with them; tell the prospect some information about you, maybe something a little personal, a quirk of yours, nothing too heavy but something that makes you look vulnerable. Maybe declare how something makes you frightened, say. This can be very powerful and I strongly recommend it. There is the need to protect in all of us. In fact, I read that now in the States when training soldiers they don't talk about destroying the enemy and being aggressive and fearless and psychopathic because apparently, this fuels regret, remorse and guilt. No, the training is about relating combat to protecting. A natural instinct is to protect.

Expression of your vulnerability makes you appear accessible, and if they don't fear you they will allow you to get close.

If you display some vulnerability people will naturally want to protect you. Our Sheila is a leader in this field. I watched her cloak herself with the guise of being a baffled little girl and observed how people then listen to her intently, agree with everything she says and forgive her everything. It works for awhile. It's part of her addiction to self pity. Honed vulnerability enables her to hijack meetings, and get endless therapy at the expense of tax payers' and those that need help and want to recover but can't access the limited resource. And breathe.

One of the most successful insurance salespeople I met had a chronic stutter. People around him would freeze and listen regardless of how painful it was and what's more, would never argue with him and would always take his viewpoint. I cite an extreme case but the point holds true.

Use your vulnerability to your advantage.

People feel comfortable telling you about them if you've told them about you. But, you should spend more time hearing about them than talking about you.

Generally it's dangerous to just start banging on about what you do without a break. The idea is to put the client in a box: in simple terms, 'if I can provide the features you've described, then you will buy today?'

Beware, better not to b@llsh*t even a bit, even at the beginning. Imagine a clear glass of mountain water, fresh, ready to drink, that's the truth. Imagine a pipette of black ink going in, that's the lie, over the period of the influencing process it stains the whole thing.

If you tell a blatant lie your prospect will pick it, but they won't challenge you. You will therefore think you got away with it but chances are you didn't, and if they continue to communicate with you it's because they are using you for information. But they will not make a positive decision to go with your big idea. They will find an excuse.

It's very hard to detect when someone doesn't believe your lie.

By the way, I'm not sure about attacking the competition or anyone you may see as a threat to your big idea, at any point. I tend to think this largely reflects insecurity. If the target is negative about the competition a small one sided wry smile might just be enough '.. ah well, not to worry I'm here now...' kind of thing. There are ways of putting the knife in, or rather planting a note of doubt but it must be done with subtlety.

Be cautious when criticising other people who may be associated with your prospect, their friends for example.

What if your target passes on a negative from someone else and you leap in defensively by decrying the perpetrator and find your prospect likes that person, now you are on the defensive. Because you counter attacked the person rather than the negative viewpoint your prospect will more likely defend and hold onto the negative viewpoint. They agree with people they like over and above the subject matter.

Rather like taking a side in an argument between married couples, it's you that's going to lose! If you make a comment about the competition, or gossip about someone, they will listen very carefully but chances are it will work against you.

Avoid being personal.

Note: if you are positive about an aspect of the competition, or someone that may be a threat, that's not obvious i.e. beyond a feature they major on, the prospect may move towards them, so chose carefully. And if you make a negative comment, or what you think is negative, they may reinterpret what you say i.e. see the exact opposite, and so, again, you may push them to the competition. In essence: your recognition of the competition signals fear; that you are threatened and the prospect assumes there must be a reason for this, a reason that may benefit them.

Use an obvious positive 'yes, new car, very nice, horse must have come good.'

Rather than: 'hmmm, I've heard he has a gambling habit.'

Essentially, if talking about the competition you are walking on egg shells. Be careful. Ambivalence is your best approach. You are neither here or there.

The perceived threat may have an obvious major, i.e. something that is prominent. Their charm, size, their marketing, their looks, they deliver quickly....so if the competition is mentioned (*not* by you) then pre-empt their obvious positive with your pre planned repose.

E.g. they're known to have a lot of clients and therefore claim popularity.

"....hmmm..oh them, well I consciously strive to be a specialist and tailor my proposition to a more discerning clientele.."
"...well I'm very particular that's why I'm here with you.'

Their seemingly positive has a negative. Everything does. You don't criticise them directly. Simply change the perspective.
'He drives a Maserati.'
'Yes, some people seem to need propping up with flashy toys, despite the debt.'

Anyway your enemy is procrastination, not the competition. The competition might be helping you, i.e. wasting their time educating your prospect and getting the client closer to buying!

Every time you re-engage with the client. Things have changed. Attitudes have changed. Re-qualify them!

Remember the: five contacts to make a decision. Whether or not it's exactly five I don't know but the point is; generally it takes a multiple of contacts....FIVE. That is not necessarily five contacts with you, it will include any other exposure they may have, advertising, an overheard conversation...

My most successful periods in business development were created because I qualified brutally. I took the attitude that the prospect and I are doing each other a favour. With any interaction you should always be ready to walk away. Whilst you need to express humility, you need not express servility; as such your target will take you and your proposition seriously. They will see that you are serious about your wares and they will develop respect for you. They don't respect the person that keeps running away and coming back with a bone/information and dropping it at their feet.

Remember my Libertine – confidence - always projecting that you *may* love them...*if they behave in the right way....!*

Let's just review a bit. Get in step with your target. Find out where they're at in the whole process. Find out what they know. That way you can adjust your spiel so it's tuned to their knowledge and beliefs. Tell them but let them tell you, and preferably let them tell you first. Get them talking as soon as you can. Stop yourself from jumping down their throat. Don't be afraid of silence, they have something more to say. Pause after they've spoken. Absorb what they say. Don't just look like they're yet another dumb person who you've kindly given some air time: that you've heard it all before. Feed what they say back to them. Show them clearly that you understand them.

That's why you can be very successful at the beginning because you're enthusiastic and your approach each time you meet your prospect is fresh. You listen and you think about your response. Your target feels like an individual.

Firstly, you need to know you are talking to a buyer/the decision maker and that they are prepared to make a decision, and have the ability to do so.

In essence: "...if Mr. Wealthy, I do this, get that, find the other, give you good reasons, you're in a position to go ahead?"

They hesitate and make an excuse then drop them, or move them into the 'later file'. Move on: you're not doing this just for a laugh. Don't feel compelled to continue putting them and you through the process. Get rid of them and create the space for a 'real' partner. Whilst you're wasting time focusing on a non-prospect the real one will fall into the arms of your competitor. Get ruthless with your time. Great influencers understand this. Don't worry too much about burning time wasters. Sift continually through your prospects trying to find if you're kidding yourself, or that you've developed a blind spot for a person, i.e. you are getting along fine, he's great to meet, chat with, he will do it one day. Remember the person that can make a decision, i.e. can actually decide and make a commitment and can pay the bill, may not be all that pleasant to deal with at first....get over it...because just spending time with the dithering nice guy will not pay the credit card debt.

This is about the qualification process. Probably the most important aspect of the process; done as early as possible. Before you push your boat out make sure you are rowing in the right direction. I'd rather ruffle the feathers of a prospect than look at a blank score card at the end of the month.

Always be looking to get agreement. In essence, getting a positive decision is about getting agreement

Don't forget, and this is critical, you are helping the client. You are doing them a favour that you are happy to do: a favour all the same. If you are going to do something for them, then they are going to do something for you. This is a two-way street towards helping them achieve their goals. You and your big idea is really good, it's going to improve their life. Get agreement from them early so they join in the journey; they become a partner. You're happy to help and do, but they must agree to be involved. You may need to be plain, firm and frank about it, albeit polite. If they are not making agreements with you they're pretending, maybe just gathering information or using you. Drop them.

".....I'm just going to tell you a little bit about the retirement home so if you want to know more later you can ask, if it's not relevant I'll leave you alone, is that alright?"

"....obviously you're not investing financially at this stage, but clearly it's our time we are committing. I'm happy to look and find you appropriate candidate for this job but I need to ask if you to always return my calls, you'll appreciate we're in this process together, we want to achieve the same objective and not waste our time. This market changes fast and to do the best for you I need your help, I need you to meet me half way, is that fair?"

Chances are, until they buy you are working for them for free. You're not their slave. Libertines that really know their stuff are often politely brutal. Some take the tack from the start that it's about moving forward to get the prospect what they need [what the Libertine wants], and they make it clear to the prospect that they are going to have to make a decision. If they detect the prospect isn't ready, they'll move on ruthlessly. Slide yourself closer to this way of thinking. Be nice to everyone or get what you want? Here's your choice 1) be nice to all and get nothing or 2) [Libertine option] batter the sensitivities of half of them and convince the other half.

Weeding out time wasters is crucial. When explaining the decision making process to them, 'I'm going to do this, and you're going to do that', i.e. narrate the process and highlight the end point. Make it clear that they are going to be asked to make a decision.

"....which is where you want to be right, eh lover boy?"

If they are insincere they will react one of two ways; either they will seem to be flippant and avoid eye contact, or they will be overly aggressive and defensive, i.e. 'how dare you ask me to make a decision'. Someone looking for change will want to help you. It's said that innocent people when interrogated by the police will be helpful, familiar and somewhat colloquial and frank with language.

'Obviously we are looking for a result that benefits us all without wasting our precious time...yes?...So what I'm asking from you is....if you want me to do this I need to ask you to do that...', trade with them.

I'm here to serve but I am their equal, no matter who they are. I am not about being subservient for the sake of it: purely because I want to influence them. People like others to be subservient. People like attention and if you allow them to keep you in a subservient position it guarantees your attention. They will maintain the façade of getting involved in your idea so that they can maintain the attention on them selves, but with your continued subservience they are happy about not making a decision. This will cost you. It will cost you your precious time which could have been more productively spent elsewhere, and it might also cost you money wining and dining. She's already engaged. He's already married.

Trade with them, don't just be servile. They need to grasp early on that you want something back, so get them in the habit of paying for your attention and conforming to your wishes early on.

'I'm going to do this for you, which is what you want, but I need you to do that...'

Remember if it's a company you're dealing with, they have an obligation to do the best for that company including buying your product. It's part of their responsibilities. No need to be subservient. Don't let them push you around. You're their equal. This applies to any relationship you are looking to form.

To get agreement you need to get in tune. I've said that it takes five contacts to make a decision. How this is proven I don't know. It's likely that a prospect needs multiple contacts before they decide. I believe that if you owned a brand new Ferrari and had a day to sell it simply by approaching people (not those in the trade), no matter what the price, you'd struggle, even if the buyer could resell it in an instant to someone in the trade for a significant profit. They'd be cynical. It's unlikely that they would have any thoughts of realistically buying a Ferrari at the time of your approach. You tell them its ten thousand pounds and it's worth a hundred thousand but they don't know you, they don't know the car, the specific model etc. They need to hear on the radio, say, that there's a millionaire that wants rid of a car, or hear it from someone else etc, this is where advertising and marketing come in.

So how far down the 5 contacts journey has your prospect travelled?

I play the saxophone (allegedly according to me). I drove 60 miles to a shop that sold a special brand. A young, helpful, knowledgeable chap worked in the shop and did a great job of explaining the benefits etc. Another older gentleman turned up. He was quieter than me, didn't ask so many questions. All three of us tried the saxophones; there were various sizes and models etc. The young chap took a few phone calls whilst I spoke to the old man and found he had driven 240 miles and he already knew everything about the brand. He had come to buy; I had come to mess about. The young chap hardly spoke to the old man and I was surprised he didn't walk out, but he was on a mission and bought one anyway. The young chap was lucky. He should have qualified me out and the old chap in. He didn't ask the old man one question and yet he wasted loads of time treating me like a rich relative with a terminal illness. On a scale of 1 to 5 on the scale of contacts the older chap was at point 4 and I was at point 1.

Simply being pleasant to people is not necessarily influencing. In fact, you may have to argue quite fervently with a prospect. Avoid getting personal, but sometimes this works. I personally like a salesperson to stand their ground when selling to me. I border on picking a fight with them, test the strength of their conviction. For me I'll respect the salesperson, believe they have integrity, plus, the prospect that scraps with you probably makes decisions quickly and is serious. If the prospect enters into a heated debate with you it's likely they are real buyers [don't get personal, focus on the issue]. But there are ways to do it.

Trick….(very powerful)

I used to argue with the prospect about an issue that wasn't especially mainstream to the big idea. Watch their hairs go up, keep at them and then eventually concede. Let them win. This works a treat. I'd do it for fun. After I'd 'ruffed' them up a bit and they've 'won' they then become my friend, they end up defending things I tell them. They feel a hint of guilt at having proved you wrong mixed with a feeling of triumph. They will have a feeling of wanting to pick you up off the floor and repair you, and part of this will be conceding to something you want from them (which is actually more important to you, rather than the silly argument you just had). Before the argument they will have had a fear of you because you are the person that is going to challenge them to make a decision and that, and therefore you, are a bit scary. This feeling is now weakened as they are less afraid of you. They feel as though they can protect themselves against you and the challenge you represent, i.e. getting them to decide and change. The reverse is true: their defences are weakened. They feel bolder and braver: less fearful of change. Good for you my Libertine.

Also, they may be wrong, they may have more to learn. But after you concede your words will have gone in and mark my words, they will change their minds at a later date, which is what you want.

Think of two boxers hugging after a fight. Somehow the combat bonds you. If things are too 'nicey nicey' and superficial it's easy for them to nicely reject you because

113

they know you'll be nice about it. Stuff being nice: the nice guy who is a friend to everyone is an enemy to himself. Get into it, dig. Break the egg.

Client... "...well no again, blah, you're wrong, blah.,.."
Libertine: pause,.... look out the window (the dawning of a new understanding)... '..ooooh, hold on, I get it, so your saying......, well, you know I never thought of it like that, I think you may be right, I should take that on board. Say, Bob, forgive me for my belligerence...."

I think it's a good idea to raise the emotional level. It gives the process more impact. It will make the prospect think more about the proposition afterwards. I read some research recently claiming that on a first date with a partner you should do something that makes their heart race. It makes you and the date more impactful.

Don't be worried about stirring the prospect up a bit. You're not going to be a kiss ass just for the sake of it. From the start, get the prospect to commit to action, get them involved, this isn't just a one way street. A lot of buyers get addicted to people making them feel important. The prospect and you are entering into an agreement. You deliver this concept politely, extracting any arrogance but you're being fair and open, and that's what you expect from them. Do this at the start. You state clearly you are going to trade with them. You will help them but they must help you. You may feel them sting a bit but they'll know you're the real thing and that you're there to get them to buy into the plan, and that's what you expect them to do. Importantly, it will get rid of the timewasters preventing you from getting into the 'pretending to influence' cycle.

Be bold and challenge your prospect's ego. Position yourself as the embodiment of their ability to make a decision: let them prove themselves to you and *impress* you with their decision making abilities.

However, watch this one. I'm speaking from a man's viewpoint choosing to challenge another man. Remember if a man is in a 'street' confrontation and there's women present the likelihood of it escalating to violence is a lot higher than having just men present. I've sold to couples and there's danger in taking sides or ostracising one. Taking sides with one causes the other to be stubborn and they become harder to dislodge from holding onto the wrong idea.

Equally as an aside: do not take sides if dealing with a couple in conflict. Just gently support the positive view not the person. It will blow up in your face at a later time if you do. They may well make an agreement in your absence and turn on you, make you the victim i.e. use you in absentia to absorb and embody the negative energy that came between them. Also, don't overdo the support of the good idea, i.e. add more energy than the one who is a proponent. The one who is in disagreement will feel 'ganged' up on and that you are the cause of the feeling.

'Yes I agree Bertie, you are completely wrong Susan, utterly mistaken and Bertie is right.'

Better: '...hmmm, there's merit in both viewpoints but others have found that what Bertie is suggesting may well be the way forward.'

Just remember if you argue with their opinions you are arguing with their pride and ego. You need to lose to win.

Back to trading - remember: it's good to get your prospect doing stuff for you from the outset. Teach them from the beginning to do things you for you and always be mindful when they do - lots of hugs and kisses for them.

'Now I'm going to go and do all these wonderful things like I said I would: all those things that we agreed would be very helpful in getting you the information you need to invest your inheritance. But what I need from you is to make sure you post the agreement back to me in this envelope...'

'..oh and you did that...oh well done that's such a help..'

People like to please and they like to be rewarded.

If they don't get involved you'll be pretending to influence them because they're pretending to be interested. Good for activity but doesn't make any money!

Summary
1. If you've not qualified the prospect only luck will make the decision.
2. Get in tune with your client ASAP.
3. Ask questions about their decision making process so far, every time you communicate.
4. Find out what they want.
5. Keep asking for their agreement.
6. Trade with them, I do this you do that.
7. Make them aware that you are there to HELP THEM MAKE A DECISION.
8. They ARE going to make a decision because you going to make them or make it for them.
9. Test their conviction/s – challenge them but don't prove them wrong!

Chapter 8
The Big Idea

"Lazem n Gem...pray silence for the pitch" da,d,dahhhh...

When I say 'pitch' that could be explaining why these shoes are so good or why they should get a nuclear reactor or why you should get a raise or why the wealthy old man should buy a woman's designer shoe shop!

You may not be a person with the 'gift of the gab'. I would bet on this being an advantage. You'll be better at listening. Most that talk a lot think that others are grateful of their presence and that they relish the opportunity to listen. Wrong: mostly the quiet folk are humouring the 'gabber'!

Years ago I walked out of a sales job after the first morning of 'sales training' about selling wardrobes. There was a scripted pitch they insisted you stuck to. Lines like, "... you look like the kind of person that appreciates good quality, am I right?". "...I'm guessing you'll be wanting to take advantage of our special offer, is that right?" Part of the routine was to actually make a dummy phone call to the sales manager to see if he could give a special discount to these lucky people providing they agreed to be a 'special show home'. Did they want me to wear a Widow Twanky outfit too? I mean what a ridiculous pantomime. 'Behind you, behind you...'. What? People actually go for this low grade rubbish?

Always treat your prospect with respect. Any condescension will come out like you are spraying paint on them.

Always be patient with your prospect. Give the information without being scripted. It's not a canned con. Go through it: step through it, like you're doing it for the first time. However, I don't think it's wise to tell people it's your first time. If you do they'll probably be nice to you but they won't buy from you. It's likely they'll be suspicious of your abilities. Like attracts like and more equals more, and you always give the impression of having done this before.

Plan what you are going to say and then improvise. Contradictory, I know.

In essence, you need to be armed with all the relevant facts. You don't want to be caught out. You always need to be, or at least appear, knowledgeable and confident about the stuff you should be knowledgeable and confident about. So do your homework. Practice; get smooth with the delivery of the key facts. But don't feel in the least bit like you *have* to deliver them. The general idea is to have an overall structure in your mind of how the spiel is going to go, littered with relevant detail, but at the same time you must be ready to adapt your delivery to the situation and the new lover. You must have gauged at the outset the style and flavour of the delivery. Be flexible and malleable, and be fresh. Make sure your delivery has that first time edge; every time. Any hint of a well worn spiel will be picked by your target instantly and they will shut down. You start with your 'canned' performance and they will retort with their 'canned' rejection.

Hey, maybe try a bit of honesty my Libertine (easy now). If some of your spiel sounds like marketing bull try declaring it as such.

"...I'm not sure I understand this [you do] do you? [you are not smarter than your client, you're the same: get them to explain it to you].

".. what do you think, does that sound like marketing waffle to you?.."

"...there again it could mean [reinterpret it],...",

"....perhaps it's open to interpretation, anyway, what's most important to you, I guess, is point that....".

This way you engage the prospect. You're not talking at them with the belief they are happily soaking it all up, rather than silently thinking cynical thoughts which is what they actually doing. You are getting them to help you find your way through.

You may even find that the prospect defends the marketing material and then you simply agree with him.." yes, that's true...". Don't be afraid to go in reverse, i.e. try going the other way round. I'm not suggesting you disrespect the material, because this will reflect badly on your idea which you are proud of, perhaps just mark it out as what it is; support material. Done with finesse it makes you look like you're on their side. What you can then do is bring their attention to a section you think is vital.

"...I know it's typical marketing bumpf/ agreement (not contract) stuff, but I tell you what, I've actually read it all and I thought this bit *is* relevant,.....I know other people, like you, have said that this bit is important......". This makes you sound like a genuine human who has their interests at heart rather than yours.

Try a line like '...I'm not sure I'm making sense here....am I? ....[pause – they'll join in]...'. You need to know they understand you, and by making it your fault (which it is if they don't) they are more inclined to volunteer that they don't understand you, i.e. declare '....I'm not explaining this very well....you'll be doing well if you understand this after that terrible explanation....does that make sense to you....?....how would you put it?...'

Don't be too smooth all the way through. You may have heard it all but it's new to them. If they don't follow you, they won't agree. Be vulnerable and they will volunteer their vulnerability by telling you if they don't know what you're talking about. If it's important they understand something, you need to know that they do. Get feedback.

NOTE: if you hand some information to people...guess what? They're going to start reading it, maybe not even from the beginning i.e. they'll very possibly start reading from the middle, but you won't know where. Also, they're going to stop listening to you. Your voice is going to become an irritating background noise; they will subliminally relegate your voice to a sound that is not significant. Talking whilst they are reading is NOT influencing, unless you are guiding them through it, therefore you need to control what they are looking at on the sheet/pamphlet/contract. Especially males; we're not so great at doing two things at the same time, e.g. watch sport and listen to partner? No can do.

So ask yourself, 'do I want their mind to wonder around gathering information from the sheet?' If you do, shut up and wait: I mean wait until they look back at you, or sit down with them and guide them through it. If you wait whilst they read you'll feel uncomfortable; compelled to say something. It is at that moment when great Libertines stay silent and wait because after awhile, which may seem like an age, your prospect will more than likely ask a question. Part of the reason for this is subliminal recognition of your patience, therefore they offer their respect by asking a question or making a comment, plus they will need to demonstrate they have read it and more importantly, they want to gain your approval. Whatever they ask is a good question. If they don't ask be suspicious, they may not be a buyer and they are simply going through the motions. If they don't ask a question or make a comment: ask them a question about the information. Get flushing for the truth, quick.

"...here..." [by the way, try handing something to someone and say that, 99 times out of 100 they will take it off you]

"...[pause]...so, rather than going through the whole [holiday brochure] lot let me just highlight a couple of things if I may....", and then lead them. Get your digits through that nose ring!

I did a presentation a while back about a complex internet software solution. The appointment had been booked over a month before. Two of us were going in and after fiddling around designing a 'powerpoint pressy' we agreed in advance to keep it all short and simple and shut up and listen; which was a good plan. We assumed that the prospect would know why we were there given that I'd called several times and toed and froed with emails and wot not. We were wrong, me especially as I was the initiator. Fortunately, half way through Sundance's spiel one person asked a question which made me realise they didn't know why we were even there. We quickly rewound right back to the beginning. The presentation was not **framed** in a context.

'Ahh ...whooaaa there Kid..we are here because....'. We failed to bring all present right up to the start line standing together side by side ready to start the story, ready for the off! We needed to start by reiterating our reason for being there: how we'd come to be sitting in front of them and the overall purpose of the meeting. We'd sent them stuff before we got there and arrogantly ('hey it's us you lucky people') assumed they had it all in the forefront of their minds.

Not so long back (2007) a famous violinist busked in a New York City subway: of one thousand that passed by only seven stopped to listen. He typically would fill the greatest concert halls across the planet!

Context. Framing. Packaging. Positioning.
Think like a sniper. Don't rush into it. Don't snatch at it. Get everything right and settled.

It's a mistake 95% of salespeople make when phoning. They call for even the third or fourth conversation and expect the recipient to remember immediately who they are, why they are calling and what they were talking about last time.

Bring the prospect up to the line; put them in the starting blocks. Remember what I said about neutralising what is going on in their minds and then introduce your big idea....remind them why you are going to tell them what you are going to tell them. Be sure they are ready to hear it. If something else is clearly nagging them, then better to rearrange for another time. The main course needs to be served up properly with the right amount of care and reverence. Set the table, light the candles and get the mood music on.....seduction, my libertine....

Whatever you are offering there will be a part of the process from prospecting to closing that is particularly awkward, akin to your market. The marketing / support material should be a weapon to help you with the difficult bit. For example, you may have plenty of prospects but there are loads of competitors and therefore you need to be separated from the crowd. Or you may have a special offering and prospects are few, so finding and qualifying a target is very difficult. In fact, this is relevant to my last story because me and Sundance were trying to sell to one of only three companies in the whole of the UK for which the product was relevant. Right off the bat we cocked it up! Forgot the foreplay! Doh!

Let's just consider props for a while. You may need them as part of your idea.

Note: marketing folk, or people that provide props that are not making direct contact with prospects, will send you out with a bunch of pozidrive screwdrivers when it's flat heads you need! Marketing people never go out and sell. They have no idea what a sales cycle is and the general shape of it in relation to the product their company provides. I know; I've met dozens. Marketing people think that selling is lesser to marketing and that 'selling is a function of marketing' – I quote a marketing manager – the rest, i.e. the lion's share of the marketing, I presume is a function of marketing and disappears up its own arse – like most marketing managers.

Be suspicious of any marketing material that has been created by someone who has never dealt with prospects directly.

Aside: I did some consultancy work for a company that made a widget for the double glazing business. Sales and therefore revenue was spiralling down despite spending a lot of money on marketing via the marketing manager with a nice company car (that remained parked in the company car park all day) and big office and secretary. According to the General Manager all installers (their market) knew of their product and that the distributors (whom the installers bought from) only asked for their product because they had a patent on it and it was superior. This was confirmed by the marketing manager. I jumped in the car with the salespeople. They gave me a different story as did the distributors as did the installers – all of whom I spoke to. The salespeople were glad I went out with them because they figured someone would pass on the truth of the situation and so end the boss berating them for the bad sales figures back in the office. The patent had run out and there were several superior, cheaper products on the market. Distributors changed staff and they had no idea about the name of their widgets. The installers: ditto. When I relayed this information to the GM I thought he was going to hit me! He did however fire the marketing manager and take my advice on a proper marketing campaign that SOLD.

It might be a brochure for retirement homes for grandma or information on honeymoon cruises.

BUT, read and re-read all the bumph if it's written material you are using / giving to your target. Even if you've been at it for awhile, it may freshen up your approach or you may find that something contradicts what you've been telling prospects all that time, something they read after you've gone... oh dear.

If you present information, control the presentation of the material. Frame the material. Put the material in context. This is what it is. This is what is important. This is what it means. This is why. Get it? Make sense?

Meanwhile back in the MiG.... I recall a story in the Cold War about an exercise in simulating battle between the sophisticated superior American planes and the then Soviet MiGs. In the heat of battle the U.S pilots couldn't use the complex equipment......I joined an outfit doing residential sales. The top gun looked real smart. His car was clean. Clean inside. His desk was tidy and most importantly, his briefcase was organised. The home improvement products had many variables. Before he went out he could dip into his case and pull out the relevant information at any time, easily, quickly, without breaking the flow of the wonderful sales waltz of seduction he was in.

Rather than bending down mumbling, "...oh, I'll find it in a minute, I'm sure it's here....errrr, now where is it....errr...., oh I've dropped my pen.....". You've lost them.

You know how that fumbling person makes you feel uncomfortable? If the influencer is a bumbler how does this reflect on the big idea?

If you're going to take the trouble to go their place or wait around for them, get organised. Right from being able to get the jacket from the hanger, say, to practising with the slide show, open that bottle of carver; get smooth. They'll notice these little things. You can look like an old hand/ pro who knows' their stuff straight away. They'll assume you are. They want you to be. They want to be seduced. They want to feel **safe** with you. It's going to be okay. How you have access to a pen that works, napkins, a book to write information down in, how you access the bra strap is SYMBOLIC of how you and how good your idea is, and what a good idea it is to agree to it!

They'll judge you on the little things. People buy houses because of things like the colour of the carpets!

Con people know this.

I can't stress enough how important this is. An extreme example would be the story of DeNiro, who I understand bought a New York taxi and drove around for dozens of hours before filming Taxi Driver. Get familiar with your props.

So, practice and always look to improve. Keep it simple. Likelihood is you'll strip it down rather than carry more. But what props (sales material/ contracts [agreements] etc) you have, you know where they are, what they are, and can access them easily in a timely fashion. Think like a smooth magician. Unless you've got Tommy's charm, chances are you haven't, why shoot yourself in the foot? Give yourself a head start. Anyway, a few practice runs will give you confidence. But don't hide behind practice, get on with it, get your nose bloody.

And, if it starts to go wrong in the heat of battle, so what?

Fumble, fumble " oo now look at me, it was all going so well, [and hear you can blither and blab a bit, it's worth just stepping through that uncomfortable silence], I don't believe this I've been practising getting this slide show going and look here, it's got stage fright...". You'll appear human and you'll be forgiven.

And then, *repeat back the bit before you stopped,* i.e. reconnect with the story and.....Tango on! Relax, you're not looking for a scalpel to chop a bit of brain out!

'..ahh got ya, anyway where was I? I was just saying that [repeat what you were saying before you stopped]'. Don't start from where you left off. Go back a few steps. Imagine you are tying two ropes together – you need a bit of overlap to tie the knot with.

"oh, it's not here, I haven't got it, no problem, not to worry I wonder if anyone reads it anyway, I'll send it over......as you were saying before,.......anyway, it's as you'd imagine [this will dislodge their mind and get their attention again, and get them believing that they would have understood and agreed with the material].."

And always present the information with reverence. Make like it contains the secret formula to eternal life. Don't just sling it over. Think like an expensive jeweller that handle goods with special gloves and put the pieces onto special cushions when presenting them. If they just tipped the diamond rings out of plastic bag onto the counter it would vastly devalue the product. It all adds to the perception of the person receiving something special.

The moral (Moral? Do what?), my Libertine, is to practice with that cloak...that reassuring swoosh..!

Know this: if your target is serious about making a decision and changing / doing something their outer critic will be on high alert. We all have an outer critic; some have a more critical critic than others. The outer critic criticises one's environment and therefore finds fault. When a prospect is getting serious, just when they are getting close to tipping over to making a decision especially, they start to look for fault because they are getting nervous and they are looking for an excuse to buckle out. So don't let them find fault with your use of props. Act like a well rehearsed magician my Libertine.

Practice. Those awkward little square packets, that stubborn flip top ....put the new batteries in?

Also, it may be that you've got into a habit of trotting out the same stuff you will start to sound 'canned'. Ask yourself when was the last time you changed it? Your gained experience on the subject will have changed your perspective.

If I've got a pitch I might even introduce it as such, they know it is so why not identify it. This creates trust; you're not trying to pull fast one. Chances are when you launch into a pitch I bet the tone of your voice changes and starts to sound 'canned'. You've practised it before and they'll pick it straight away. The pre-rehearsed pitch sticks out and that prompts them to play their part, i.e. the 'target' that sits quietly thinking of a reason not to buy. If you slide into a canned story the seller-buyer two step begins. If you identify the pitch then they become your ally; 'we're in this together..'.

"...I've got this information to [regurgitate] to go through with you, if I may.....to be fair there's a few points it's best we look at,.... so you know what's what,.... so we've covered all the bases if you like.., does that sound reasonable?...". Keep it chatty.

'...hey, whilst we've got a bit of time, how about we talk about whether or not we let them switch off the support machine for your dear old wealthy auntie...?"

Again, try narrating the presentation of the big idea. Tell them what you are going to tell them and at the end, tell them what you've told them. This makes you appear open and frank and therefore creates trust. Don't be ashamed about being convincing, don't try and slip things in, be open about it. You're there to influence, they are there to be convinced and that's the point of the whole exercise.

'...I know how you feel, we all want her to keep going, but where is the dignity..?'

And don't present loads of information. Keep it simple. Simplify it all and then take some stuff away. And I don't mean taking loads of stuff with you and only showing them some of it. If they see there is other stuff to see which you are not showing them they will be suspicious.

'...look, I took the trouble to get this lovely brochure...this urn with the flowers on...she'd love that..'

I did business development for an ad agency. I was a master at presenting the creative ideas. I would work out who, or rather whom, was [were] making the decisions and make sure they were all at 'the' presentation. There was a lot of build up, investigation and preparation before this point. I would take only six boards. I've read that the mind struggles to hold more than seven issues/items at a time [numbers for example]. I stayed safe with six, no more, no less. I had a special portfolio case to hold them in (they were big). I would always clean the case and make sure nothing was inside except for the boards (with the relevant pictures on). I would put the boards carefully in order. I would check through the order several times before I went in to the appointment. I could picture them in my mind and rehearsed exactly the points I was going to cover in relation to each board before I got them out. I would even position the zipper exactly in the same spot every time so as not to fumble. My hands were manicured. I took out each board with reverence after a short build up, after positioning the whole meeting at the start, after re-establishing rapport. I had worked out the dominant people and separated the 'kino's, the visuals and the auditories. I would lower my tone. I would shut up and listen and I would watch them, not the boards. I would notice every facial move. I would wait. I would let them touch and hold and own. I would not push them to an early decision, I would let them swim from idea to idea picking up how they were thinking and feeling. Which way was going to be the idea that 'they would choose' (which I already knew!). I would nod approvingly at positive comments and stay frozen at negative ones. And at the right moment, which I got an instinct for like a leopard crawling through the long grass, I would strike; or rather herd them into the decision. If necessary 'tell' them. 'That one is you'.

They don't want to hear your pitch? Ok, what do they want to hear? What do they need to know? You chatted with them, you built rapport, did investigation... Your story may get jumbled up but it shows you're listening and tailoring to their needs. If they ask for specifics you flag sections in your mind, i.e. bits of the story you'll miss out or emphasise, or even jot down notes on what they want to hear and near the end you summarise, checking you've not missed anything. Or maybe they put you off giving them the full spiel: so rearrange. But you can summarise what you want/need them to hear at the end.

'...oh okay that's fine Mr. Moneybags...I just wanted to tell you about the returns, was that something you wanted to know?.....oh, the capital investment was more important....'

If the timing isn't right, i.e. they haven't got much time or are in a rushed frame of mind and you feel that the offering needs their full attention – don't shoot your bolt.

'....well it's better we sit down and go through this one, you need to understand everything fully, I'll pop back..'

Back to the story...it's on!

"..we are big and therefore have the resource to help you...we are small and therefore flexible...".
Imagine a third party asking them to answer in a short sentence what the positive is about your big idea after you have left. That short sentence is what you need to program into their minds.

'errrr we're dead expensive, rubbish product but the salespeople are really good looking and anyway the narcissist greedy boss needs more money and the lads back stage couldn't care less....', that sort of thing.

'...yeah I know he's bankrupt, unemployed and has a drink problem but he has a nine inch tongue and can breathe through his ears.'

Join up the dots for them and keep it simple. If there is a positive say why it is a positive and then pause. Let the positives go in. You may even want to change the tone of your voice at the important bits – lower it a bit – makes the positives serious, or inject a little enthusiasm. You may also add a gesture...remember the NLP. Try *'anchoring'* the moment. Just as a moment of positive enthusiasm passes by, a moment when you can see that your prospect reacts in a positive fashion, e.g. laughs, or enthusiastically agrees with you, then make a gesture. The gesture can be anything, but not a gesture that gets lost among others or used at another time. You could touch their forearm (be very careful with touching), or simpply put your hand up a little in the air...anything to *punctuate* the moment. If you do this a few times you when the ambience is exactly the same, i.e. positive, you will be programming them. When you make the gesture again it evokes that positive feeling in the prospect; that enthusiastic feeling that you want them to have. You can then use the gesture at a time when you want them to tip over and make a decision. It helps to get them through the concerned anxiety. You can also use the anchor the next time you meet them, this way they will feel positive in your presence and they will associate you with feeling good.

Important: you have lived with the big idea for sometime. They have not. Their mind is whirring around, especially if they are getting close to making a decision – *they start to panic.*

If they interrupt you to ask something this is good, even if it's jumping ahead. Repeat the question back in a slightly different form (don't mock) if you can.

".so you're asking......you're right, that's important, I plan to cover that but, if I may, let me just cover off a couple of points first.....', you can use this technique to ensure you maintain control of the path of the story, and then you can chose to go back and answer the question, or give it the swerve. Or, answer the question but be aware that when they interrupted they may not have been listening to some important stuff you were saying (too busy waiting to interrupt), and so after answering go back to the thread of the story...with an overlap, i.e. go further back than the point at where you left off.

You need to cover off the foundation stones of the opportunity. You have to be flexible and tailor your story but don't skip the fundamentals. It will be hard to go back at a later date. And when I say fundamentals, I mean establishing credibility for example. Plan in advance the main points that you need to get across.

"...ok, I see, let me,...before we move forward... if I may, just summarise....[then cover the main points and get agreement]....".

"..yes, good question...it's important to you to know x, what I'll do *if I may*, is say what I'm going to say, cover off the basics and we [joint journey, you and the prospect] should get to those points you asked about....blah, blah into the story....and [later] here's the point/x you asked about....[or even] *may I* ask, this is important because...[pause and they'll tell you]...ok, so if I can show you how the part share in the diamond mine works then we're getting towards where you want to be?...[get a close on it]."

Prospect "..it's important because..."
Libertine: "... so if it's got the certificate of authenticity, that's what you are looking for?" [close, shut up]
Libertine: "..well we can provide that because...blah, blah, [there's a company in India that prints them]."
Or, "..I'm an early riser and can drive you back to your place so you can change for work.."
They have ratcheted nearer to the deal.

The story must engage with them and their situation. It's not a standard recorded message where you leave it to them to choose what is relevant or otherwise. Don't natter along expecting stuff to stick.

But at the same time it is important to maintain control. Think method acting. You both start at one point go through several phases and then arrive at another point.

133

The phases may get a little mixed up, or they or you, may swerve off path, but always be aware of this fact and keep gently steering back.

Client waffling on 'Blah, blah, blah....'. Be patient. Keep listening. Let the fish dive: pay out the line.
"...hmmm, that's interesting, by the same token ..', and then change back on path.

This is 'box' influencing, i.e. ensuring all the bases are covered off so the natural path of least resistance is toward agreement. Imagine the sheep being blocked off so they move into the pen. If you don't cover off the bases they will escape. If you miss an important issue you will pick this up when you summarise, it may be the very first bit about the company say, or an important feature of the plan, go back and get it out.

"...well thank you for your patience, just quickly if I may, I'll just run over the points we've covered but please, if there are any others let me know ok? [always getting agreement].."

"..I hope I made some sense, are there any issues we haven't covered?" [then shut up]

"..you asked about the..blah...did I answer your question...so you feel comfortable with that...?"

If there are two or more people involved in a multiple contact proposition try and project yourself into the conversation they are going to have [even in their heads] after you've gone. You DO NOT want them asking each other what you were banging on about, or asking each other why you didn't talk about a certain issue/benefit/feature. You will be amazed how many people will sit through a pitch and be afraid to ask about something they need to know. Squeeze it out of them.

"...to be fair, I live with this concept although it took me a while to grasp, does it makes sense, please say if there's anything you don't understand....[silence]"

If they've bought in their mind: if they agree with your proposition then they may not have to hear the entire blurb, so shut up and move forward with the plan. Otherwise you'll buy the idea back off them. You may well go and say something that puts them off; puts doubt in their mind. Some would be influencers insist on going from the very start all the way through. Your prospect maybe at contact number 4 when you meet them, find out where they're at and take it from there.

'You can't buy it now you fool you haven't heard about the blah, blah.'
'Oh, but I don't want a blah, blah, you know what I've changed my mind about the whole thing..'

I tried to buy a kitchen recently, it was hard. I went in to one place for the third time (what?!?... I'm a compulsive kitchen shop visitor?), after waiting at the counter and being ignored I wondered around the showroom and a saleslady whom I hadn't met told me all about the benefits of a particular kitchen. She knew her stuff; the doors could be put on a curve, "like this you see...", and this top was great, the best one because of, well, all sorts of reasons. She could talk. She had a great voice, nice tone; she was smart, explained things really well. I asked her about her sales experience when she finally paused. I was intrigued. She'd been a teacher. Ah (likes the sound of her own voice?). What she didn't know because she didn't ask was, a) I'd been in several times and had been sold (by myself) a particular style of kitchen, but now, given what she said, I was beginning to question my judgement b) my kitchen is straight therefore no need for curves, and I was in a bit of a hurry c) the top I'd chosen was different and I realised I needed to investigate this issue further d) I'd just come in pay a deposit, I actually had my cheque book in my back pocket, which I didn't use. I thanked her for her help and left. I bet she thought she'd done a great job of selling. I noticed another kitchen selling place appended to a DIY store at a later date. I knew what I wanted (I was at point 5) and the sales person closed me down. I bought. The sales prevention officer at the first place had successfully stopped me. Moral: if you're talking, make it relevant. Otherwise my Libertine, stick to looking deep and meaningfully into their eyes and purring in wonderment..!

Remember: Improvise. There is no set pattern. EVERY time you tell the story it's different. BUT...with every big idea there are basics to cover. With improvisation the musician uses a scale of eight notes. With method acting there is a start point; basic points to get to and a set end point.

Don't forget when you're telling the story; they may be in new territory. You are not. They need time to understand, grasp and absorb. Be patient. Tell them what you've told them; better, tell them what you've agreed. Almost as if you work for them and you are deciding with them. You're in their corner, not the opposite one. Be their advocate.

The set pitch has a purpose. The person who scripted it has more than likely gone through the main elements of the product and packaged them so that you can trot them out. But influencing is not painting by numbers, it's about controlled improvisation. It may well be important that you get the main elements out; they are the foundation stones of the big idea e.g. your credibility, the credibility of your company, the history of the product, the team etc. Do not assume the target knows stuff. Be delicate about presenting what may seem obvious to you but may well be new to them.

Talk about 'painting by numbers'; I recall not staying long doing business development at an agency that specialised in wasting the marketing spend of charities by not getting much in the way of results. For some historic reason they had a big charity on board so others used them too (herd safety). I had to do a double call with the boss and the chap we visited actually said that the only reason we were sitting in front of him was because my (cold) call was so good. When we came out the boss 'told' me to write an exact script of the call so that others would be able to read it out when phoning prospects and get appointments too....! He had everybody walking around carrying their cups of coffee (drinks) on a tray in case of spillage and the in the tea room everything had to be in size order, among a stream of other neurosis – I heard a rumour that he used to climb over his neighbour's fence and steal her underwear – any correlations or signals...?

Aside: your enemy is not the competition. It's a) your incompetence, b) inertia: the prospect's unwillingness to make a change and, as such, the fear of making a decision (decision fear).

Narrate the process. This is very powerful as I've said. Never be condescending, for example....

"...so that's that, you look like the kind of person that wants 20% discount, great quality, 18% return, am I right? ...I'll just call my manager and see if we can arrange it...."

"No don't, just sod off."

If you look carefully you'll see your prospect bite their lip, touch their mouth; they were about to tell you how to convince them but you had something better to say. If the client appears to want to say something, let them, even if it drifts from the main stream of your mentally pre-designated story. The fish has the hook in their mouth, let them dive, pay out the line, let them go down and wind them in again later, don't try and stop them. If they have an issue let them get it out in full technicolour.

If interrupted don't start from where you left off/were interrupted; get their mind back in tune. Same goes for those annoying folk that butt into the office or the noisy child that enters the room. It's almost as if you have to pick up the thread in their minds which has snapped at the interruption and then you tie on the new bit. So, repeat the last bit you were saying and then carry on. In other words, after the interruption don't immediately start with the next bit of the story. When their listening is interrupted the last thing you said gets erased, you need to put it back in their head.

Libertine: '...yes the thigh bone is connected to the knee bone and the..'
[interruption] "Bob, I bought some new suspenders.'
Libertine: 'Yes Bob, the thigh bone is connected to the knee bone, and the knee bone is connected...'

And whatever you do, don't show even a glimmer of irritability, you must have endless patience for a prospect. Make sense? [close]

You don't know something? You'll be amazed how people will cover for you. Open honesty is so disarming; the prospect will help you fill in the gaps, reassure you rather than attack you for not knowing. BUT it maybe something you should know. If you don't, for goodness sake get your ass back and learn it. You should always be learning about your idea, it keeps you fresh.

"[repeat question back/clarify/get them to expand]....that's a good point...may I ask what makes you ask that? Is it because...so you're saying...."

If it's a point that's not been raised before it could be telling, it could be an important part of the decision process for them. It may be that they have a false pre-conceived idea about your product which needs digging out. It may be that they're just testing you, filling the air. Or the issue they've raised may be critical to them and thus far you haven't dealt with it – now is the time.

Remember.....very important......if they're asking questions they are sending buying signals – they are tipping over. If they are asking then they are buying in (especially if it's about the price).

Don't panic... '...you know what, that is an obvious question, but you're the first person to ask it....and I'm embarrassed to admit, I don't know but I'm definitely going to find out because I should know, I'll learn something myself....then I'll get back to you...".

The important point is: get back to them. Arrange when you will and in what format, and then do it *before* the agreed time (exceed expectations – separate yourself from the crowd). How often have people said they'll get back to you with information only to give an excuse at a later date? How do you judge them? You want to appear reliable and therefore…safe.

[Aside: make the above lines your own]

I've used lines like this to great effect. I never go to meet a prospect worrying whether or not I know everything. It never hinders my ability to influence. In fact, I've sold immensely complex systems knowing very little. BUT, the 'little' would be the BENEFITS!!!

Don't forget, it's not about listing features; it's not about listing the most technical aspects of your product. If you're describing a technical feature you must focus on the benefit. The why, the 'what is it for', the way it's going to enhance the new owner's life. You are not drawing an architectural blueprint; you are painting a picture of emotions.

"..so the inverter processor is great because what it means is your staff won't be claiming compensation because they've got themselves burnt...makes sense doesn't it?" Pause. Translate any feature of your big idea into the 'what's the point of it', and slap a close on the end, i.e. nail it down.

Maybe wait some more. Get them to absorb it in their minds (they'll probably dis-engage eye contact if they're absorbing information; so shut up and let them). Let them translate the feature into a way it will benefit them. Often if you wait long enough they'll tell you what that benefit is, your silence will provoke this. Let them talk it all the way through whilst you nod approvingly at them. Even say that you'd never thought of that benefit, or heard it put so clearly....

"...that's right you've got it.." (approval).
"...that's a neat way of putting it.." (flattery).

You may even use their phrases to help another client take possession of your idea. You'll be amazed how a client will give you ideas that you can use next time, and if they cite a benefit – they're buying, they're taking ownership.

"...so, what I'm trying to say is, this new material means this coat is waterproof and robust, ideal for your walking trips to Wales wouldn't you say..."

"...yes, like you, the last chap got one because he needed a coat that he could rely on..."

"*you've got it*...no more complaining from Bob./.. and as you say (reinforce something they said)./..yes that's a valuable point which I forgot to mention..../ *like you say......*", and here you use their language.

An advanced technique is to outline a benefit and stop half way through, relax, pause, lift eyebrows; they'll either make the mental effort to complete the sentence in their mind i.e. program themselves, or they will actually say the rest of the benefit out loud. Then give them a gentle affirmation, "exactly, you've got it, ...', or simply nod and smile. People want approval. Less is more.
'..relax yourself on my supersize sofa and watch that romcom, have a cognac and then....'

I do a lot of improvising. When young musicians improvise they just keep playing and playing. Think Mile Davies. Play a note and shut up.

When I'm pitching I steadily change my tone. It starts relaxed (here's some new stuff to learn but let's not panic) and fun. Then it becomes more formal (your purchase is a serious issue – I take you seriously), and then becomes softer; I'm looking to seduce my clients, weave a web over them and possess my prospect. I keep maintaining eye contact. I keep my hands in full view. I use steady pauses. I nod. I speak slowly, clearly. I ask for agreement without necessarily pushing for a response.

So in summary:
1. You can narrate the pitch, it breeds trust (nothing up your sleeve).
2. Have fun with the story. Mix it about. Keep it fresh.
3. You want them to interrupt you; it'll tell you what they're thinking.
4. You want them to make you jump to a given part, out of your sequence; it tells you what is important to them.
5. Be brave, every pitch situation is as individual as a snowflake. Let it be so.
6. Summarise. Ensure you have covered the key points/benefits.
7. Tell them what you are going to tell them, tell them & tell them what you've told them.
8. Keep looking/asking for affirmation.
9. Part of you beckons from the end point and your other part takes the journey with them.

Chapter 9
Getting a Yes

I recall being told that the person hardest to convince is not the person who keeps offering objections, but the person who doesn't.

Aside: when I say 'objection' I mean raising an issue that appears as a criticism but appears like a reason not to agree with your wonderful idea.

More than 25 years ago in my early sales days I had to take the boss on a call; usually the death of a sale. Typically, you'll find the boss having not been out of his ivory tower for a long time and is hindered by imagined, preconceived ideas about how his product is being received and also, insistent on establishing his dominance in the meeting they will undermine your credibility. The prospect sees all this and the net result is they think less of the proposition. The prospect can be embarrassed for you and somehow they put you in their camp as 'us vs the boss', as a consequence the sale drops down the gap. There said it. I'm not much for two person sales calls [more], especially not with the boss.

Keep the other amateur away. That ripe neck is yours my Libertine, no room for two sets of teeth!

But of more relevance: we were selling computer solutions and in the car on the way the boss drilled me not to talk about a particular issue, which on sitting down at the meeting he promptly did. '...I must admit I nearly bit my tongue off...' he said on the way back. But that wasn't what worried me. I'd visited a few times already and felt I should be seeing other people at the organisation other than just this one person. I was right. If your big idea is a complex solution get other decision makers involved. You'll meet happily with one person the first time but not the second, same goes for a proposition for households; get both/all decision makers in front of you. If you haven't, make sure you've got some more information to go back with, like the price. In a solution proposition (complex) it's a drip torture process i.e. getting interest, identifying decision makers, getting in tune with them and then getting them in tune with you, but always leaving yourself room to go back to them, having something to go back with. For example, you give some of the decision makers (just the husband) all the material and information to make a decision....

'...great thank you for all the information and the presentation, I think that about covers it all...'

'...so is it something you want to get involved in?' [close]

'...well I've got to talk to Queen Alexandra about it, obviously, she writes the cheques, so I'll let you know.' You're dead. You will then forever be chasing the sale, leaving messages etc, you've lost control.

Anyway, back in the car reflecting on an awful meeting where the boss trampled all over the situation. He was one of those types who was absorbed with being 'the boss', i.e. it was about his ego rather than facilitating the success of the organisation. The idea of asking me for an update on the progress of the potential sale thus far before the meeting endangered his authority, and so he didn't and was therefore pre-equipped to undo all the good. He knew best because he was the boss: that type! But something else was nagging me. I'd only met this one person in the

144

*organisation. In my heart I knew something was wrong.
I'd kept the whole thing afloat; it was potentially a big
sale, a proper company. I'd invested so much time I didn't
want to even think that the whole thing would derail. One
can get into a deluded state. But my instinct told me that
given we had spent time together travelling down the sales
process, which creates pressure, i.e. the moment of
decision is coming closer, he hadn't raised any 'issues',
he hardly asked any questions. It was too smooth. I was
young and felt uncomfortable challenging an older,
seemingly senior chap.*

When people are about to make a decision they panic.
People don't like making decisions that's why they keep
doing the same things over and over. If you, or anyone
else, are about to make a decision it will affect you
physiologically. For sure, particularly if it's a big decision,
your heart rate will go up. When people are getting close
to a decision/moving towards the tipping point, they begin
to raise more objections/questions. This chap didn't raise
any. I also left with only the option of being able to call in
hope of picking up the order, i.e. I had shot all my bullets
and therefore I was already dead. The sale didn't happen.
When I called to 'pick up the order' he'd left, I pushed
through to the General Manager who informed me that he
had been 'let go'. I appealed to the GM suggesting I had
spent a lot of time there and deserved, out of common
decency, some sort of explanation. Apparently, this chap
had a habit of this; he simply liked people visiting him and
making him feel important. I actually found where he
lived and called him. I was annoyed with myself mostly,
and wanted to find out what was in his mind, which
wasn't such a good idea, after a short conversation I
realised he'd had a mental breakdown getting sales people
in to pitch at him was part of it. But it never happened to
me again.

How many dates have they been on?

What did I learn? 1. Qualify hard. 2 A solution proposition/ complex idea? = several buyers. 3. A complex solution? = always have something [information] you can go back to them with. 4. You learn most from your mistakes. 5. I want objections.

NB In short: objections are good. The process is getting traction.

You're telling the story and they raise an issue. If it's an objection that's awkward don't panic, don't say anything, drain it out of them with silence and don't feel obliged to counter it, say nothing, just pause and think about it. They're expecting an immediate counter so they may be ready to parry your response by defending their objection like a reflex action, and in so doing hold tighter to their objection. The more they defend their objection the more it will become a belief; then you've got problems. Just think, they have this thought now but it's changeable and you're going to make it easy for them to change that thought without any discomfort, or damage of pride. So, if they come up with an objection, good, they're serious about making a decision.

Give the objection space. Contrary to your instincts, they grow stronger with immediate attack. They weaken with space and time.

Some objections are more important than others. You don't need to tackle all of them. Better you don't. Why? Because subliminally you will program them to believe that you will have some sort of answer, be it good or bad, to everything, so they will stop objecting and therefore, stop buying. And you may well appear like a Smart Alec no-all/irritant. You're not there to prove how smart you are – we've already agreed that you're not, remember?

"..okay,[pause].. I understand..[.look like you're thinking about it, repeat the objection back to them], so you're suggesting that...it's a fair point... it's a relatively common thought ... I see, that's understandable...you're not alone in thinking like that...that's an interesting point [and then, IF YOU HAVE TO, counter the objection i.e. come up with the answer BUT DON'T make it up]..", and then return to the pitch, but repeat the last bit you were talking about.

The point is: you want to encourage objections...get them out...they are the bad apples...so reward them for giving you objections: make it ok.

What if you're interrupted with what sounds like an objection?
"...our company is relatively young"
"..so you've little experience then?"
"..little experience...[use the repeat technique above...]...oh, you're saying that it's a new company so we've not been in the market long?..[This buys some time during which they may well be thinking of a counter to their own objection.]...fair enough, it's a valid viewpoint" [make the objection a 'view' it's not necessarily their belief].

".. our new company makes us flexible and ready for the new market terrain...the senior management are a team that have 900 years between them.... sooo, the company is relatively young and fresh, as I mentioned...", i.e. return to the pitch at a point before they interjected...pause, get everything reloaded back in their minds.

"...our company is relatively young and therefore created and operating given the flexible needs of clients today, as part of the natural evolvement and improvement in the market...".

An objection will tell you a lot. It tells you what is important to them. It tells you they are listening and thinking about your big idea. An objection tells you that they are thinking about taking on board your big idea. They are getting closer to making a decision and this scares them...good.

Lots of "ummhmmm, makes sense....good point....yes, often asked and a genuine concern... interesting, may I ask why you ask that...?". Feed the questions back, "... that's important to you because.....?"

Again, this buys time and may prompt them to answer their own objection. Note: if they object and look away chances are they are thinking out loud and will answer their own issue, so shut up and wait. If they look at you after asking then try the above.

"... forgive me [powerful phrase] this 'bit/your issue' I'm not confident about an answer to that...."

[the subliminal message by default is: I am confident about the other information I gave you, and because I declared a lack of knowledge, I tell the truth, as such I believe in what I'm offering and I'm a decent and trustworthy]

"... but I'll find out by Tuesday and get the answer to you [it gets there by Monday, yes?]...".

In short, declaring vulnerability implies a person worthy of trust. You can't know everything; in fact you don't know much, they don't either, remember.

Here's the manipulative bit: If when speaking they are reinforcing the positives of what you are saying, and often they will, raise your eyebrows and nod. Everybody seeks approval. If they're raising objections I freeze my face and look carefully at them, holding their eyes, I may even narrow my eyes a little at one point during their objection and say nothing, just frown slightly. I don't tackle the objection. I stay silent. Don't be tempted to jump down their throat.

"what!...no, no, no you fool, I'll put you right Mr Prospect, haven't you been listening, surely if you were to engage your brain Mr. Prospect the answer to that would be obvious...oh not this objection again, what you too, listen will you, I'll say this once and once only and then I don't want to hear anymore of this whining...". This is the message that jumping down their throat offers. Result?

Like I said, say nothing....they will probably then handle the objection themselves, they may just be thinking out loud. So let them think it through and when they answer their own objection smile and nod. You may be tempted to say 'That's right' i.e. reinforce the positive.

But when you get really good you won't say anything. You will stay quiet with a small Mona Lisa smile whilst just nodding ever so slightly you will be looking deep into their eyes thinking positive thoughts about this wonderful person. And they will be buying...gliding to the tipping point...'Now there's a good prospect aren't you?'...Then they will either ask you a buying question, like 'when could you deliver?' or you will pause some more and start

149

off again: from before where the script broke in a low, easy tone...you see, Mr.Prospect...objections are nothing to worry about....together we can manage those can't we?

Aside - (here's my dirty secret). If a prospect is giving me positive feedback I look into their eyes and think of them as an innocent child, which they once were, and think 'you are a beautiful person and I love you.' Just for a brief moment. Perhaps with a husky 'that's right'. They pick it. How is it that we turn round and look straight into someone's eyes? A lot of communication is unspoken.

I use this objection handling technique the most. Nodding and smiling slightly when they say the right thing and staring, frowning slightly with eyes narrowed when they don't. It teaches them the best path of thought, the line of thinking that gains approval, remember we all want approval. You're training them how to behave and what to think by giving them your approval, or withholding it from them as you chose.

That's why 'seduction' is in the title.

Want to be a Libertine extraordinaire?
Read this: at the end, when they're asking lots of questions, what are you going to do? [Rhetorical]. They are getting close to buying. In fact, you don't want to be countering every objection that comes up. They are just fretting, their heart rate is up.

Ever tried water skiing? Your instinct is to pull yourself up with your arms. You'll stand up quick and then fall over. So don't, sit back, keep your arms straight and keep the rope between the skis the boat will pull you up.

When they're asking lots of questions, they are about to buy; they've reached THE TIPPING POINT and your instinct is to jump on each one. It's just the neurosis phase; you naturally want to jump on them, pressure them. No sit back, control your self and breathe deeply and steadily. You're getting nervous too, you're going to get a decision, serving to close the match, just the keeper between you and the goal in the 91st minute; you're going to score the winner! Stay calm. Say little. The process has its own momentum now and it doesn't need pushing, they just need gentle reassurance. Calm your voice, take that quick sharpness out, speak more slowly, put your hands openly where they can clearly see them, you're not hiding anything; you have done this 100's of times before. Long pauses before you speak, in fact if they hurriedly voice an objection, don't speak, gently tilt your head to one side, wait; feel the pressure of the pause. They'll be compelled to fill the gap, the spouse may answer the partner's objection, or the senior member of staff may take this as a chance to assert authority with the answer. They'll handle the objection. They'll answer their question, they already know what they want to hear and, they want to buy. When they do, respond to their own objection, nod approvingly and with a good pause, "yes, that's absolutely right [then gently lead them], pop your moniker on the agreement [not contract – too scary], there… and we can get that all sorted …here I'll get your coat and we'll get going..".

But maybe apply the close after handling a barrage of questions, or at least three or four.

Of paramount importance: the one most powerful thing you can do to influence people and it's often very hard, and   some   find   it   impossible, it's...ssshhhhh.....the power of silence......you can apply enormous pressure by applying silence.

Hold your nerve. Frantically batting back each question will aggravate the situation. Play calm doctor with patient about to have surgery. It's going to be okay. Don't snatch at them, picture them slowly swimming into your net. And it's worth bearing in mind, its proven that if you speed up your voice you speed up their heart rate and therefore create a feeling of anxiety which is the opposite to what you want. Slow.... down..... your..... speech. When I am closing I go into slooooowwwww, mmmoooottttiiooooonnnn, even my movements. Maintain eye contact transmitting positive, loving thoughts. Speak clearly, softly, no 'errrs'.

Maybe you chose to pile the objections up. Make a mental note of each or write them down. Even suggest that 'we'll look at them in the end', maybe what you have to say later in your pitch will answer some of them.

"..that's a good question, I'll tell you what *may* I carry for now because I'm going to get to that point...'.

There's a chance that countering each objection as it pops up begins to derail the process. So you need to readjust so that you can cover off the bases. Sometimes digressing from the main story is good, the prospect is only half listening waiting to cover off an issue that is important to them. Conversely, be careful not to lose the control you need, in essence stick to the recipe, i.e. don't let the prospect pull the whole thing out of shape, i.e. irretrievably away from the overall pattern of your story. Make sure you go back and deal with objections if you can, or at least be aware of those not dealt with; they may fester if you don't and they may kill the deal in your absence. Alternatively, if you want to take the risk don't bother, which saves on countering them, especially if it's just irrational neurosis: your call.

Note: if the objections increase in frequency they are leaving the situation/the mental state they are in and going into a new one: they are about to make a change, a decision, they are about to jump. This for most is scary. They are tipping over. They may come up with a few irrational objections at this point. You've got to find your own way, your own style.

You can acknowledge the situation if it gets a bit much. Without mocking.

".... It's perfectly understandable, I'd feel the same, most of my dear friends do at this stage, it's a change and it's disconcerting [they will catch themselves; become aware that their late objections are no longer valid] but look, we've done this before, we fitted one just like this, remember we talked about it, remember how I told you about.. [reassurance]... let's move forward, we can get you booked in for Next Monday or would you want us to get cracking on Friday [get their minds focused and moving forward with the alternative close]....". They may fall off, ask more questions, "..but, but...what if....", stay calm, super tolerant, go back round again, they'll wear down. In fact, that feeling of fear will exhaust them, and with you staying calm and reassuring them it feels safe to accept your proposition. Going with you becomes easier than resisting.

So resist your instincts to speed up towards the line: pull yourself up on those water skis. Slow down. Ease off. The process has its own momentum, let it pull them in like the boat pulling you up.

Maybe after a barrage of objections with you staying calm, answering a few, gently closing here and there, there will be a pause, their eyes may glaze or they look away, you stay quiet, they are letting go, they are tipping over, they may even nod with resignation or sigh or smile, they've stopped having those thoughts of resistance, they've tipped, they've bought. But at this moment of outward stillness created by a buzz that is inside of them they are unlikely to be able to say, 'ok I'll do it': you need to lead them. So keep smiling at them and gently nodding, then gently.

"...would Tuesday or Wednesday delivery suit you better?"

AND THEN SHUT UP!!!!!!!!!!!!!! YOU SPEAK YOU'RE DEAD!!!!THE DEAL IS DEAD!!!!!YOU SPEAK AND THEY HAVE AN OUT....

Swoosh with the cloak and in with the teeth!

Being able to see them tip is an instinct you can develop. They may tip the moment you meet them, or you may have to use the Columbo close [more] as you walk out the building. It can come at any moment. Be ready for it and if the basics of the deal, the building blocks, are there so that the deal sticks, let them buy when they are ready not when you allow them, and the easiest way is for you to shut up and watch and listen for the signals.

When they tip over they relax filled with a sense of resignation. They go into an almost euphoric, dizzy state. That's why con people will get away with short changing them. Keep calm. Your instinct like the novice water skier is to get excited and speed up and force the situation. Wrong, do the opposite. Speak slowly and clearly and move slowly and project to a point after this very moment, lead their mind.

I was in central London the one rainy evening. A mother and two children looking slightly bewildered were standing by the road. A cycle taxi pulled up and asked if they were looking for somewhere. They wanted a particular theatre.

He asked, "do you want me to take you there?" Like the shop assistant, "can I help you?"

To which they responded? "Errr, no thank you." Parry.

What if he'd said in an easy confident way "hop in out of the wet and I'll take you..". Tell them.

Talk them over the tipping point. Tell them to move forward. Don't leave them staring the big decision in the face, keep their minds moving forward, not jarred at the decision point.

Don't ask them if they want to jump. Just gently tell them to jump. Trust me, it's what they want.

So, frequency of objections/questions increases. Handle a few and then get a close in, i.e. one that targets beyond this moment. Relax. When they have agreed/responded to the close....keep moving. They have resigned to the decision. They have bought so keep the momentum going.

'Okay, if you just now follow me...'

'Ok I've noted down red for you, so let's do this..'

'...good call, welcome aboard, lets just get the paperwork knocked over and then we can get you enjoying the excitement of your new helicopter...here just pop your...'

Keep control of their minds. Tell them what to do. They can't think. Don't ask them complex open ended questions. Just give them simple choices 'a' or 'b'. It's like they are hypnotised.

Buyer's remorse is likely to hit them at some point... 'Oh what have I done....I've gone and made a decision....there's going to be a change...oh dear...'. Don't let them wobble, keep dropping questions (simple & unrelated), comments, phrases in front of them to keep them moving forward. Like those pieces of clothing in a trail to the bedroom!

Always know what you are going to stay – or more powerfully – tell them to do AFTER they have tipped and agreed....

Objection [silence].Objection [counter].Objection [silence]. Objection [reassurance]. Close [silence]. Lead & Tell....

'So which do you prefer red or green..' [minor decision close]
'Green' [they've tipped and bought]
'so all you need to do is pop your credit number here...'[lead them & don't stop, keep leading]... 'that's the way...and all we need to do is pick a date for delivery, say next week early or later?'

Always, always, always have the route down the tunnel to your lair planned out. And practice leading them. Once they've tipped and agreed DO NOT just stand there and not know *exactly* what to do and say next. DO NOT even look like you are trying to decide what to do next. If you do they will be desperate to ditch the deal: make like the money is in the car and not come back.

And after the detail is all signed up.

'So have you got transport to get you back?...Did you see the weather forecast..?'

Get away from the decision. Start them talking about a benign topic. Their minds have gone gooey. Their bodies have flooded with adrenaline then dopamine. They cannot think rationally and therefore you need to get them away from the agreement they have just made before they wobble. So, have a planned topic ready that you can easily slip into that does not tax their minds.

Again, if they say yes DO NOT just look at them aghast in silence, or look overly delighted/ surprised and then flap about panicking.

Handling the price and offering discounts can be a challenge.

"...and as it happens we've got some discounts,... hey what a surprise [join them in the cynicism; it neutralises it], but [slight pause] to be fair, they are a seasonal thing and will run out in June, just worth bearing in mind, I'm just covering myself really if I didn't tell you might be upset later ...".

" ...you'll understand I'm showing you a product in the quality end of the market which is, to an extent, reflected in the price, you get what you pay for and all that, you know how it is [there you've said it, it needed to be said and then pause, they may reinforce what you've said, then move on]..".

"...how does that phrase go..? Something about paying too little being a false economy...or something...you regret paying too little rather than not enough...." make these phrases sound like you've just thought of them, it's likely that your prospect will help you re-phrase them, great, she now owns them, and she's with you.

"oh yes... that's the phrase I was looking for.... you've got it...", almost flippant. If all is okay play your hand with disarming honesty.

"..it's like this Mr.Prospect, we're in business which is fair enough..., we're keen to stay in in operation...if we don't survive and therefore can't look after our clients [mould this as you will],... it's as you'd expect, there's all the overheads including me so, moving ahead tonight that way I can pass the saving on,[pause, nodding]....... let's do it [tell them, and it's us, we're doing this together / follow me].

'...Mrs.Prospect, we do it now I can give you 10% right off the bottom, yes?' Shut up and nod. They may say nothing, they're thinking. They're at the tipping point . No movement, no objections, no sound? Wait a bit.

"...what would you prefer a Saturday or Sunday delivery?" [alternative close] delivered in a soft easy tone.

"I guess Saturday would be better.."
"Morning or afternoon?"

Bingo! Then gently move into taking the order (more).

Think about your big idea. Start at them agreeing with your idea and think backwards. Lure them to the decision rather than push them. This is what happens when you get good and have bitten a few necks. Think about the moment when they are going to verbally commit. Make it easy. Give them a small decision to make which presumes the big one.

'So would you prefer the delivery of it [the jet fighter] on Tuesday or Thursday?'

(You know what? A lot of the old stuff in influencing has been around for good reason! The benefit being: once you can influence people you can have anything you want!)

How about that blunt honesty? Give it a try. You don't have to wrap everything in cotton wool and cheese. You don't have to disguise what you doing or be ashamed of it. This methodology works well if you've built a strong rapport, i.e. you've somehow bonded, or at least, found some common personal ground with the prospect/future happy client.

"..ok, I'll say this because it needs to be said [change tone, you can be more forceful or *lean in and lower your voice and be frank, always maintaining unwavering eye contact* – this technique applies to handling any difficult subject], there's a cost involved in me being here, I come back for whatever reason then the cost increases. I'll be blunt if I may, if we move forward now I'm authorised to give you 10% [you don't make the decision, it's from a higher authority and therefore non-negotiable]. The 10% leaves with me, I know that sounds like high pressure nonsense, it's just a fact [said clearly with confidence]. There it's said [palms out, shrug, pause]. Anyway, ...' and shift back to the tone and manner you had before. They've got the message dirty business dealt with, and back to happy stuff.

You get the idea. Make it your own, practice, adapt.

Say it like you are saying it to yourself. Some stuff needs to be said, the price issue for example needs to be tackled, the quality highlighted, but you're not dealing with a five year old so cut the condescension. Present like you are presenting to a good friend. You genuinely don't want them to miss out.

Note: when talking about the price – bags of front (confidence). Never, ever behave or speak in a fashion that may be interpreted as shame when it comes to the price….the *investment.*

"…I'll ask you to forgive me for saying this, I'm your friend remember, but the fact is this discount won't last, we won't need to discount in the winter season, IT'S AS YOU'D EXPECT.." and then link on to the next bit of information.

I could rant on about the power and the meaning of this last phrase. I knew a successful chap who lived off this line alone. The fact is, the prospect takes what you've said on board and they circumvent their own cynicism.

"It's as you'd expect...." I used this line to great effect when selling air-conditioning sometime ago. It was a seasonal product and I wanted the discount to create sense of urgency. I'd be clear and frank about the discount. It was important that they recognised the significance of the discount, so it was openly laid on the table for them to accept. It wasn't presented in a cheesy fashion.

In the summer we didn't need to offer a discount (it was a hot climate), there was plenty of demand. They got discount in the winter but the discount started high in autumn and got less and less. I explained this frankly and clearly.

"..and just at the moment we're offering a special discount..[so what? maybe the product is always discounted]'. If there is a reduction in price at that time there must be a valid reason and to get it; the prospect must trade with you, i.e. it's cheaper now because....but you have to make a decision now...and it won't last.....and be sure it doesn't – word gets out.

Aside: remember you're not an emotional needy type looking for reassurance. Some questions/closes do not need to be answered out loud. Think of the comedian that is amusing, but you don't necessarily laugh out loud. Isn't it irritating to be forced to respond to cheesey questions? Let them simply answer it in their minds, particularly if the answer is obviously yes.

"...our product is the lightest on the market, which is what you want I guess [slight pause, no need to drive a response from them] because obviously it's lighter to carry on to your private jet..."
"...okay I get the sense you are interested but you may feel that you need time to think about it [slight pause], you want to get it right [avoid 'decision', too scary] ..how does the concept stack up..is the timing ok? [close]. You feel okay with the quality?[close]"

Note: question them down near the end. Go through the main elements of the story in a list. Either get agreement on each, or dig out issues/objections and separate the problems from the big idea, i.e. weed out the problem/s and separate it/them from issues they agree with so the problem doesn't infect the whole deal. Get under their skin: dig down for the problems.

Don't: "so what do you think to the idea...?"
This invites...
"I'm just not sure about it, I need time to think...",
you've then got a wrestle on your hands, (i.e. don't ask their opinion on the whole thing, *ask about specifics*).

From here on you're chasing them: at that very point they have dodged the net. But, if you go through each element you build the story, you put them in the box. You put one of the sides on the box each time they agree to each element. If there are any problems dig them out. If you don't want to hear the specific problems you will be letting the prospect off the hook. A voice in your mind will tell you its okay to let them go. You tell yourself that you haven't pushed and been offensive and, as such, they'll call you up later and give you a 'yes' (they won't). In effect, you are colluding with them and putting the moment off: giving them an out. You're deluded.

There's a brutal phrase, 'all buyers are liars...', which is to an extent true. They have a 'routine' worked out in their minds which they [prospect] are ready to trot out and some of it may not be the truth. They neglected to mention that they are bankrupt. They are single when they are not.

What if it's a one hit deal, i.e. no re-visits, and you can't handle the objection. Try the silence technique, but if they're still glaring at you find out how important it is. Is it a deal breaker? Try and lessen its significance. Are they just looking for an excuse not to make a decision? Dig.

"...so you're saying [repeat objection, pause]...how important is that to you? Would you say that it's more important than say [match it against something that is more important that your offering has]..'
'...would not having a lift mean you wouldn't buy..?' [you should have already investigated and found exactly what they are looking for so this objection shouldn't be a rational reason to stop the deal. So their answer should be 'no', and they will they start to reject the objection themselves]..

'...I understand, it is an issue but in balance you are getting the sea view' [something better].

Or make them aware that life is a compromise sometimes.

'No you're right, it hasn't got gold knobs, but we agreed that not having gold knobs was not a deal breaker, or more important than having brass handles, which it has,...sometimes, *as you'd expect,* one [we've all compromised at some point Mr. Target] has to compromise a little to get what you want...'. Get over it and move on Mr.Prospect. Be a big person now...

Isolate the offending objection and separate it from the decision.

A builder said to me.

"..there's cheap, quick and good...you can have two.."

Sometimes you've got to be blunt and frank about it. Shocking people into reality can sting them. But wasting your time and you not feeding those seven dwarfs will prove worse when you feel the sting of Snow White's tongue lashing!

It's rare that you meet someone and they are perfect, or that a dream comes true. We all know this. If they want something you should find out at the start what they must have, or at least what they think they must have. If you haven't got what they want then make a call, maybe it's 'ding next', quick as possible. Or challenge them, especially if they've been looking for a while. Get them in reality. If their resistance is emotive and irrational, i.e. they are deluded, think about moving on; don't get determined to convince them as I have tried in the past: made it a challenge for my willpower - wrong. Get out and get another prospect. Or, bring to light that it's potentially unreasonable; maybe they need a verbal slap into reality.

Great Libertines are never afraid of doing this. A good virtual slap round the chops will bring them into reality: wipe that deluded grin off their faces. You know it's what they need!

"..he said he'll leave her for three years now..."

The method with objections is to isolate them so they don't infect the whole proposition.

Let's talk about buying signals; sometimes mistaken for objections.

It's amazing how people miss them, often again, because they think that each prospect should go through the same process from start to finish. Some prospects are at point 4 when you meet them and some people move quickly through all the points, so if a buying signal comes up, jump on it. Forget about the routine you have fixed in your mind, let them get on board with the big idea for goodness sake.

An agreement signal is usually in the form of a question: it's almost like a closing question that you would ask them.

Ever been to a market over in the Morocco?

"How much is this bracelet?"
"Do you have the same but in green?"
(with either of these questions: you've bought)

"Is all the software included?"
"Have you got one with a sun roof?"
"Are you able to deliver before the end of the month?"
"Where is my deposit held?"
"It's all kept in a safety deposit box, is that a problem?"

"Yes my son put the cash under the floorboards for me, can you lift them up?"

"Are your sheets Egyptian cotton?"

This brings us to closing. A 'close' is a question which answered positively either moves the prospect closer to agreeing, i.e. gets them to commit, or means they will buy.

'Always be closing'. There is truth in this. Arguably from the moment you engage with the prospect you are trying to move the prospect closer all the time to the deal, always asking for the agreement.

"Hello Mr Prospect, if I can explain why our product is the best and the most suitable and the investment [not price – too negative] is comfortable for you, will you go ahead to-day?"

"I understand it may be early to ask but…if we can understand the information here then will you have enough to make a decision? Start another family?"

"..if we could get it in green/add the software/get a sunroof would you go ahead today?" [close]

A bit clunky, but better than just sticking to your spiel of information. I've mixed handling objections with closing because an objection, in a way, is a buying signal and when handling an objection if in doubt, add a close. May as well, what do you think?

There are final closes which if answered positively means they've agreed. If you've got the Kahoonas you might not wait until the end you might, after establishing rapport, close them right at the beginning.

"..if after the presentation you're happy, are you in a position to move forward to-day?"

By the way, after a close of this nature SHUT UP, you speak, you're lost.

Or at the end.. "...now we've been through the detail and your happy with the company, the product and the investment, we can go ahead to-day?"

Also, and I've put in a few of these so far, keep tying them down on the way, i.e. during the pitch.

"..make sense..?"
"...happy with that..?"
"...kind of thing you are looking for?"
"...isn't it?"

The theory is that you should be creating a 'yes' frame of mind, i.e. adding a tie down at points where the prospect is bound to say yes. Go easy on this. It's worth doing but not excessively, it becomes noticeable and irritating. Perhaps just let them say the 'yes' in their heads when you try a *tie down*, unless you're looking for affirmation that they understood what you're saying because it's important.

Don't keep forcing them to say yes. They'll get the feeling of being a teenager been spoken at by a teacher – they'll shut down and start to feel a sense of defiance.

Either way, a tie down clicks the ratchet towards the agreement. *Wouldn't you say?*

Another is the alternative close; a favourite of mine. I've talked about it already, earlier or later. Why? In the heat of battle it's easy to deliver and it works. Like Bruce Lee I believe said, he doesn't fear the man who knows

1000 different kicks, he fears the man who has practiced one kick 1000 times.

"..will that be cash or card?"
"...do you want automatic or manual?"
"...do you prefer green or red?"
"…shall we take your car or mine?"
"…winter or spring wedding..?"

I like the alternative close; back to keeping things simple. In the heat of battle (MiG) they're easy to pull out of the hat.

"...so which flag would you have on the yacht, union jack or royal navy?"

Psychologically they step over from not owning into owning; they tip over. Making the small decision assumes/consumes the big.

If making an appointment on the phone I use it every time.
"….I'll spend the time, come and see you, explain what's what, Tuesday, or Wednesday?...Ok Thursday is better, morning or afternoon? Ok..2ish or a bit later?"

'Cash or credit, left or right, long or short, morning or afternoon, 10am or 11....'. Give two alternatives. Again, that's old school but its good stuff. The idea being that they make a small decision and the big decision is made by default. I ask their permission, they're tempted to say no. What? Put them in a position where they're going to have to make a decision, oh dear me no. You did all the permission asking and qualifying at the beginning, now I'm telling. You [Mr. Client] said you wanted this or that, you agreed to it, now you're going to get it.

Closing takes practice. Most do it clumsily and it's an art that you can get rusty at if you're not out hustling on a regular basis. In your early days try closing questions frequently rather than hardly at all. Better to come over as pushy rather than passive. You've more chance of making the deal for a start, and in time you will develop an instinct. Gently tie down with appropriate painless frequency, just edging them along and, if you're observant, you'll see them go into that reflective phase when they need a little mental space during which you'll be quiet, even if you stop speaking mid-sentence. Then they will ask a buying question, and you'll gently strike with the decision close and then stay quiet; get the deal and then maintain momentum by simple alternative close questions steering them towards paying up, and then a gentle subject change – and then cash in your chips.

Libertine (L) '...yes well blah, as I said..blah, handmade, blah, best quality, blah, since , blah.'.[watching the prospect, they look away – they've stopped listening]...'.

Silence, mid sentence even, and wait. Pressure them with *silence.*

Prospect (P) 'I really like the design, do you have any green ones?..'

L 'you seem, like me, to prefer the green...'

P 'yes I think I do...'

L 'would you prefer delivery this week or next?'

P ' can you do this week?'

L 'follow me, let's sort out it out and book it in. Is that cash or card?'

P 'Card.'

L '..ah, there we go,' [click clack with deft well rehearsed use of the machine], ' wise choice may I say,' or, just before the machine, 'what say we pop in the matching hat, that'll look just fine..', keep the buying going...

Then change the subject...

I know some great influencers who always close very aggressively right from the start. They tend to push people away and they may not be great at building rapport BUT they will find decision makers and they WILL get decisions and prospects take them seriously. If in doubt, close fast and early.

By the way, when the target agrees to the big idea try not to look to gleeful like "whoa, that's a nice bit of commission/inheritance for me!"

Apply more of an easy smile and keep things moving. You've practiced what you are going to say and do when they agree so it's easy and smooth: like you do it all the time. Plus, before you meet play your 'after yes' procedure in your mind programming yourself with success, like the athlete. Make agreement a path of least resistance rather than an uncomfortable experience. Buyers regret is always waiting in the wings i.e. "have I done the right thing?" and if you take the order in a clunky fashion they immediately feel regret. When people say yes, they are relieved but they also go into an unusual, hyper sensitive state. I think the rational part of their mind switches down, almost as if they get a kind of tunnel vision; it's almost as if they become slightly drugged, confused almost, so take gentle control and keep leading. It's in this state that they will carry on buying, when you can add on other peripheral deals, if you're smooth they are under your spell!

I'll contradict this completely. You can make sales by simply telling them rather than always asking. It won't work every time. Only certain people can do it. You have to really know your stuff; you've probably been in it for years or you're a truly naturally confident person (miles away from arrogant). You can ask them what they want. If it's what you've got you can tell them why yours is best. You can openly point out faults (vulnerability, shows confidence it takes them by surprise and they don't bother looking for more faults plus they will often cover over the faults for you), you can openly tell them about the competition, the good and the bad. You can tell them why the price is as it is and that it is non-negotiable (it must be). Then you can tell them to buy from you, plain, clear, firm and polite. But, you have to be talking to a qualified prospect. Ranting on from the outset is just that.

What I'm trying to say is people don't like making decisions and that's what you are going to do for them. It could be a con, that's down to you but hopefully you're genuine and you have integrity. And, you tell them to buy, to agree and do it. Otherwise you're just educating them; without telling them to say 'yes' you have given them the chance to dither – and that is what this person is used to doing and then NOT doing it – they play safe!

"....that looks like you, I'll wrap that one for you, what about a tee shirt too, here this one, put this one on.."
"....It looks like we've covered the ground, let's move forward, here you take these, I'll give you that, you pop your monikor on this, scribble your name on the agreement and we'll get on with it we can get started on Friday..."
"...you may as well pop and do it now, I'll wait for you, its' done then..."
"....this will work for you that's clear, get that agreement back today, you've done it, now you can get on with other stuff...."

"...get this one, you'll love it..."

"...look I'll be point blank blunt, this is a great opportunity, I know this business, just take it and have done..'

Try it. Tell them to what to do. It's often what people want. If they don't buy it you've done them a disservice, you've failed them. Tell them to do it. If they resist then that's good, you'll get an objection.

It doesn't always work. If applied too bluntly.

I got on a massive run selling advertising campaigns for an agency specialising in the IT arena. I had some background in this, I'd sold computers. With success came confidence. With confidence came arrogance, then the fall. I did a presentation in front of a panel. I hadn't pre-qualified the environment. I went in all guns blazing. Told them what was what, lectured them on branding, the market, how great we were. I thought it was done deal. I actually did know my stuff but my approach was wrong. I did know the market, probably better than anyone else representing ad agencies at that time, we were very creative, practically creative, we would increase sales. When I called to casually pick up the order for the extensive advertising and marketing campaign the chap said "..well actually Greg, we like to think we know something about selling printers too. I'll be frank Greg, we've gone with someone else...". Winded. I learnt a lesson. I was arrogant, that turns everyone off, I did present the best creative, we were dead good but I preached AT them. They chose second best and I let my team down. It was my ego's fault.

I should have asked permission to give a short introduction "...to be frank, it gives us a start point but ultimately, what I want to do is ask you questions and find out what it is you're looking for. Find out if you have any ideas or thoughts about how you want the marketing to progress..".

I could then selectively have disputed, or rather highlighted, alternative views based on my experience "...which I express by way of giving us the opportunity to look at all viewpoints.." and then give it to them. This would have established my credibility rather than arrogance, shown them that my team could add value rather tell them how to do their job.

Even better, why didn't I suggest to their spokesperson that I had another appointment with a 'delighted client...(calm down..).. 'nearby next week, it's flexible, just popping in to check a few things, is there a good place for a bite to eat round there. Hey, let's meet up....' Get yourself a 'coach' on the inside (perhaps the subject of another book about business development). The coach being someone you've seduced who can give you an inside track on the way in.

Moral: Yes tell them, but ask them first and find out.

Ever walked into a clothes shop and a sales assistant, if you're lucky, has said "can I help you"? What was your answer?

When I was 16 selling in clothes shop on Saturdays I'd eye up people coming in the door. Boys with mums were buyers. I'd be sidling up and doing something nearby, straightening some trousers or something, just listening and observing. Not just marching up and delivering the standard lines.

"yes those have a polyester mix so they're hard wearing and easy to iron,........it's trousers you're after? Here, try these....",

"…..that's a new design already proving to be popular…what size are you, 30? Here we go, pop these on…"

".. try these and these, I'll get a jacket that goes with it, here go over there and try them (tell them, take control)"

"…take them, they're you, here look at these, they match, this tie, shirt, hamster cage, diamond ring, blah…..".

Get in there when they're buying, keep it rolling. People think about booking a holiday just after a holiday, going to the theatre after just coming out, giving to charity, again, just afterwards.

Further: telling your prospect - once you try it and see how effective it is you may well go around telling all your prospects. You might not bother with all the fancy closes, you just point blank tell them. It works especially well if you've built rapport. If you're going through a bad patch, give it a go – get bold. She who dares wins!

"….you know what…you should buy this, you know it makes sense."

"…you were born to own a Ferrari, that's clear, get one."

"…this is you, buy this."

"…take your clothes off you know you'll enjoy it."

Tell them. You'll be amazed. It works. They want it.

Tell them. Keep a firm, straight, matter of fact face. Don't flinch. Keep eye contact.

Sometimes we want to be told, all of us. And remember you're the confident Libertine so deep down they suspect you know what's best for them (and don't you just).

Just the other night I watched a programme about buying houses. The female presenter is a great salesperson, she doesn't put up with any nonsense. She's there to sell but within that she is genuinely out to get them what they want given what is available. Particularly, the other night before the 'victims' embarked on their journey they admitted they had decision paralysis, which happens to all of us, the fact they acknowledged this is a step forward, "..hello my name is Alky and I'm an alcoholic..". Once they acknowledge their situation: the state they are in, it can be dealt with. The house hunters actually declared that they 'wanted to be bullied and told what to do…'.

The couple ran their own businesses, one each. They were spending £1million, so in effect decision makers that ran their own lives. The presenter went through their wish list, which held contradictions, she bluntly informed as such and found the best fit then told them to buy it and they did, and they were grateful that she told them, they said so.

I drove away from a village in the Cotswolds I visit infrequently disappointed that I didn't 'let myself' buy a coat in a shop there. I'd had my eye on this type of coat for some time. In this shop, they were less than half price and they only had two. I knew I wouldn't see this again. One fitted perfectly. But I'm tight, although I couldn't tell you how much I have in my current account, certainly not within the cost of this coat. My rational mind took over. I didn't need one, I've got coats so surely it would be a waste of money, be rational Greg and walk away. The whole time a young lady had chatted me up a bit, and if a young girl shows interest in an old chap he's putty. If she had just said "buy it", I would have. But she said nothing; I was even a bit angry with her afterwards.

"..ok, well thank you, I'll think about it.."
"..ok bye..."

'I'll think about it'. Which means what? How many times have you said that and gone back and bought, verses left and found a reason not to buy, or bought elsewhere when another salesperson has nailed you down? 1:4 ratio at least.

Your time, your life, is the most precious thing you have. The objective of your time with your target is to get them 'happily owning your idea'. But you didn't, so who's fault is it. It's yours because you didn't TELL them to do it.

So what is there to think about? You are never again going to let them off the hook. Don't be afraid of breaking through some sort of unwritten protocol, some accepted social moray, the sales/buyer two step: the dance of indecision.

You said this is what you're looking for isn't it, Mr. Prospect? Is it the quality? Is it the price? Is it me? What don't you get? [question them down]. The prospect owes you. They need to give you a cast iron reason not to take your idea which you should have weeded out in the first place. You may argue that this is pushy and perceive this as a negative. But the Libertine that pushes here will get more than the one that doesn't. And if you accept the philosophy that if they don't buy, given that your big idea will enhance their life, you've failed THEM, therefore it is your role in life to push! FULL STOP.

Tell them. 'Get on with it, take it / do it". BUT you have to know in your heart that this is the best thing for them.

175

"ooh okay then..". Then you will see them relax. They've done it.

"cash or card?"

I was in recruitment and got really good at it eventually after much heartache. I'd placed people with a selection of companies that had worked out well. I got to the point where I could phone decision makers up and they'd take the call or actually call me back.

"...I've just had this candidate in....not being recognised at her company....she'll go quick I'm telling you...you need to see her....I'll send her in, Thursday or Friday?...no, I'm serious, postpone your meeting, you need to find room for this lady.....no, I won't send it, she'll bring her CV in when she comes." I didn't even send the CV first, and I couldn't be bothered with any silly objections!

My hit rate was enviable. I virtually worked part time but made considerably more money than when I was humbly and gratefully typing up CV's when I started, sending them out to people who often hadn't the authority to make a decision, or was deluded about who they were looking for.

In time I began to qualifying the prospect and the candidate very hard and get their agreement/telling them how it was going to be, i.e. what I would do for them, and in return what they would do, e.g. call me straight back after an interview or when I left a meassge.

When I became successful at personnel it was about the qualification. I would send candidates who I knew could do the job, but the most important thing was that I knew the person fitted the culture, an emotive thing.

Anyway, the direct approach I call bulldozer selling. It works.

The Libertine that takes this approach will beat the one that is simply just nice every time. BUT you do have to know your market and it must be the best thing for the prospect, because your delivery has to be loaded with *certainty*.

Back to closing.

On to one of my favourites; The Columbo close. It's a tough guy close, one that can wrestle a no decison out of the bin, and it's just plain fun to do. I've used it many times. The name of the close is copied. Columbo was/is the name of a detective in a programme called... Columbo! He largely investigated murders. He would have his main suspect hemmed in, usually in their environment. He would ask them a series of questions. His manner was great, often asking 'permission to ask a question' and suggesting he might be 'missing something', and to 'his way of thinking', and say something which would provoke the target; send their heart rate up. He had a humble, approachable manner. The suspect would feel he[Columbo] was on to them, but they would get out of the hot water with their answers which he would seem to accept. He would make to leave and then turn round and put the tough one to them, the one that gets the confession. He would build up the tension and then seemingly let them off the hook and when they relaxed, he'd turn round and get them.

The Columbo close works in getting agreement. Remember I mentioned the indecision dance. There is an unwritten agreement between the Libertine and the prospect, 'you say this.., I say that,'. Each plays a role to an extent. Your prospect will relax at the end if they've managed to put up enough of a barrier to making a decision and think they are going to see you off. Or maybe you've had a meeting where certain issues were discussed but the one you want to deal with wasn't, by design, mentioned. Or even, you got the deal and you want to add something on. In these circumstances try the Columbo close.

You go through the song and dance. You've not sold. You let them off the hook. They will feel relieved; they don't have to make a decision. You get the conversation on to neutral ground, another subject. They may feel sympathy for you because somehow they've beaten you. They soften up. On the way out; I've even pulled it just before going through the revolving door or whilst being led to the lift. Whilst on the neutral subject you include a point/question whilst seemingly, innocently chatting.

"...actually, just thinking, when you said...did you mean...because..."
"...you what!..oh no..., did I ask you...?."
"....how foolish of me, you know what? I forgot to mention the ....."

The best place is near their door, or even when you are standing up ready to go because then you can get things going and sit right down again. Also, there's a bigger chance that you'll get under their skin. Their veneer has dropped and they may be more frank with you, even let their good grace slip which is good, don't be phased. Even if you don't get the deal, or it's a multi visit process, at least turn on them and get a concession, to agree to see you again, to accept your call, to look at some information.

Stay in the meeting as long as possible, without being a total annoyance. The longer you're in the more chance of getting a positive decision, or getting clouted, well at least getting a result!

By the way : if you're offered a drink, take it. *Always accept hospitality*. Unless you think they have an agenda in which case, *think*.

People often want you to take responsibility for making decisions for them. Even at very senior levels where the impact of the decision is significant. Presidents need the counsel of others.

People buy with emotion/sentiment and justify with features. People make decisions based primarily on irrational emotions. At the core of those irrational emotions is the need for safety.

Summary

1. Learn the objection handling routine. Clarify, expand, question significance, counter, close
2. Always be closing. Close early and often. May as well.
3. Always be looking for agreement.
4. Objections are good.
5. When closing, stay calm and shut up.

I do hope you have enjoyed reading this book my wonderful Libertine. I hope you find it offered a lot more than lightweight, sensationalist, speculative ideas: that there is a good deal of substance included. If there are parts you don't agree with or moreover have upset you, then may I suggest you look at these issues, perhaps they offer lessons? The book, at the least, gives you a framework from which you can operate and you can be confident in the knowledge that you are armed with the right tools.

The night dawns and the coffin lid is creaking open. It's your time now my Libertine. It's time to get what you want. Get out there and use those new sharp fangs of yours, you are worthy! Know that it is what they want. They want to give you what you want. All you have to do is decide what that is!

For me now life is about being involved in something bigger than me. My friend challenged me, or to be fair reassured me, that I would find a way of packaging a subject that people want to ignore but affects us all directly or indirectly, and is a scourge on humankind.

Childhood sexual abuse (CSA).

I am a CSA survivor.

It is widely accepted that as many as 1 in 4 females and 1 in 6 males are sexually abused as minors.

Sexual abuse traumatises the child. It stays with them for life.
The effects include: paranoia, shame, suicidal thoughts, compulsive behaviour, addiction, low self worth, depression, anxiety, disassociation from feelings,

isolation, self-abuse, guilt, dysfunctional relationships, inability to trust....there is very sadly a long list. Many of which I have endured. Before I finally had a break down and fortunately reached out, I always believed it was not 'if' but 'when' I would kill myself having fought with depression all my life – an often overwhelming sense of doom.

I have since had the privilege but also heartbreaking experience of spending time and sharing with many survivors whose lives have been so deeply affected by childhood abuse.

The ACE report (US based - Adverse Childhood Experiences) led to the conclusion that eradication of childhood abuse in America would reduce the overall rate of depression by more than half, alcoholism by two thirds, and suicide, IV drug use and domestic violence by three quarters.

'THINK'

Non minus cruore profunpitor qui
Spectat quam illie
Que faci

He who observes spills no less blood than he who inflicts the blow...Lactantius

You are now beyond step 1, at least.

Abuse of children is done in secrecy and requires secrecy to thrive. To not listen, to not say, to not stop is to be complicit.

'...shhh...' no more.

Printed in Great Britain
by Amazon